Everyman

Everyman, I will go with thee,
and be thy guide

Goethe

Translated by JOHN WHALEY

and

Introduced by MATTHEW BELL

King's College, University of London

EVERYMAN
J. M. Dent · London

First published in Great Britain in 1998 by J. M. Dent
This revised edition published by Everyman Paperbacks in 2000

J. M. Dent
Orion Publishing Group
Orion House
5 Upper St Martin's Lane
London WC2H 9EA

Typeset by Deltatype Ltd, Birkenhead, Merseyside
Printed in Great Britain by
The Guernsey Press Co. Ltd, Guernsey, C. I.

British Library Cataloguing-in-Publication
Data is available on request

ISBN 0 460 88212 0

Contents

Note on the Author, Translator and Introducer

JOHANN WOLFGANG VON GOETHE was born in the self-governing city of Frankfurt am Main in 1749 to prosperous middle-class parents. Having trained as a lawyer, in 1775 he moved to the petty principality of Sachsen-Weimar, where he spent the rest of his life in a succession of roles as companion to the Duke of Weimar, *maître des plaisirs* to the court, chief minister of the Duchy's government, director of the court theatre, and adviser on political, educational, and cultural matters. He is the pre-eminent figure of German literature, at home in all genres. His literary reputation was established by the historical drama *Götz von Berlichingen* (1773) and the tragic novel *The Sorrows of Young Werther* (1774). His plays *Iphigenia at Tauris* and *Torquato Tasso* re-established the genre of the verse drama in Germany. The novel *Wilhelm Meister's Apprenticeship* was one of the first German 'novels of education'. His life's work, the massively rich dramatic poem *Faust*, was published in two parts in 1808 and 1832 (the year of his death). His greatest achievement, however, is a vast body of lyric poetry. His interests also included the visual arts and the natural sciences.

JOHN WHALEY is a former Civil Servant, now retired, who studied German at University College, London, and at Tübingen University. He has also translated Goethe's *Poems of the West and the East* (*The West–Eastern Divan*) published in a new edition in 1998 by Peter Lang AG, Berne.

MATTHEW BELL read Classics and Modern Languages at Balliol College, Oxford. His doctoral thesis was published in 1994 by Oxford University Press as *Goethe's Naturalistic Anthropology: Man and Other Plants*. He is currently writing a book on psychology, literature, and philosophy in Germany from 1750 to 1830.

Chronology of Goethe's Life

Year	*Life*
1749	Born 28 August in Frankfurt-am-Main to Johann Caspar and Catharina Elisabeth (née Textor)
1750	Sister Cornelia born
1753	Grandmother gives Goethe puppet-theatre for Christmas
1755	Renovation of Goethe family home
1756	Begins to learn Latin and Greek
1765	Leaves for Leipzig to study law

Chronology of his Times

Year	*Cultural Context*	*Historical Context*
1749	Buffon, *Histoire naturelle* (to 1788)	
1750		Witch-trials abolished in Prussia
1751	Publication of the *Encyclopedia* (Diderot *et al.*) begins (to 1772)	
1755	Lessing, *Miss Sarah Sampson*	Lisbon earthquake
1756		Seven Years' War (to 1763)
1759	Schiller born Voltaire, *Candide*	
1760	McPherson, *Fragments of Ancient Poetry* ('Ossian') Rousseau, *La nouvelle Héloïse*	
1762	Wieland's translations of Shakespeare (to 1766) Rousseau, *Emile* and *The Social Contract*	
1763	Winckelmann, *History of the Art of Antiquity*	
1764		Coronation of Joseph II as Holy Roman Emperor in Frankfurt Proscription of Jesuit order in France
1766	Goldsmith, *The Vicar of Wakefield*	

Year	*Life*
1768	Serious illness and return to Frankfurt
1769	Interest in Pietism
	First collection of poems published
1770	In Strasbourg to finish law studies
	Meets Herder and collects Alsatian popular songs
1771	Awarded law doctorate
	Götz von Berlichingen (published 1773)
1772	At Imperial Law Courts in Wetzlar
1773	Cornelia marries
1774	*The Sufferings of Young Werther*
	Faust begun
1775	Engagement to Lili Schönemann (broken off in October)
	Travels to Switzerland
	Moves to Weimar at the invitation of Duke Karl August
1776	Friendship with Charlotte von Stein
	Interest in geology
	Begins *Wilhelm Meister*
1777	Cornelia dies
	Travels in the Harz

Year	*Cultural Context*	*Historical Context*
1767	Lessing, *Minna von Barnhelm* and *Hamburg Dramaturgy* (to 1768) Wieland, *History of Agathon*	
1768	Winckelmann dies Sterne, *Sentimental Journey* Gerstenberg, *Ugolino*	
1769	Wood, *Essay on the Original Genius of Homer*	Napoleon born
1770	Hölderlin, Wordsworth, Beethoven born	
1772	Coleridge born Lessing, *Emilia Galotti* Herder, *Treatise on the Origin of Language*	
1775	Lavater, *Physiognomic Fragments* (to 1778)	
1776	Adam Smith, *The Wealth of Nations* Lenz, *The Soldiers* Klinger, *The Twins*	US Declaration of Independence
1777	Kleist born	
1778	Voltaire and Rousseau die	

Year	*Life*
1779	Travels in Switzerland
	Iphigenia at Tauris (prose version)
1780	Becomes Freemason
1782	Ennoblement
1784	Discovers *os intermaxillare* in humans
	Launches Montgolfier hot air balloon in Weimar
1786	Leaves for Rome, via Verona and Venice
1787	To Naples and Sicily
1788	Returns to Weimar
	Begins living with Christiane Vulpius
1789	Son August born
	Torquato Tasso
	Essay *On the Metamorphosis of Plants*
1790	Travels to Venice
	Venetian Epigrams (published 1796)
	Faust. A Fragment
1791	Study of optics
1792	Accompanies Duke Karl August on campaign against France
1793	Present at the siege of Mainz
1794	Friendship with Schiller

Year	Cultural Context	Historical Context
1779	Lessing, *Nathan the Wise*	
1780		Judicial torture abolished in France
1781	Lessing dies Schiller, *The Robbers* Kant, *Critique of Pure Reason*	
1784	Diderot dies Herder, *Ideas on the Philosophy of the History of Mankind*	
1785		Diamond Necklace Affair
1786	Mozart, *The Marriage of Figaro*	Frederick the Great dies
1788	Byron born Kant, *Critique of Practical Reason*	Convocation of French States-General
1789	Mozart, *Così fan tutte*	French Revolution begins Storming of the Bastille
1790	Kant, *Critique of Judgement*	Abolition of the nobility and civil constitution of the clergy in France Joseph II dies
1791	Mozart, *The Magic Flute* Mozart dies	
1792	Rossini born	Louis XVI deposed Alliance of Austria and Prussia against France Cannonade of Valmy
1793		The Terror Execution of Louis XVI
1794	Fichte, *Theory of Science*	Execution of Robespierre

Year	*Life*
1795	*Roman Elegies* *Wilhelm Meister's Apprenticeship* published (to 1796)
1797	*Hermann und Dorothea* Begins work on *Faust* again Travels in Switzerland
1798	'Year of Ballads'
1800	Translations of Voltaire's plays
1801	*Faust I* substantially finished
1803	Mme de Stael and Benjamin Constant in Weimar (to 1804)
1805	*Winckelmann and his Century*
1806	French troops occupy Weimar Goethe and Christiane Vulpius are married

Year	Cultural Context	Historical Context
1795	Schiller, *On the Aesthetic Education of Man* Wolf, *Prolegomena ad Homerum* Keats born	Treaty of Basle
1796	Schiller, *On Naive and Sentimental Poetry* Hufeland, *Macrobiotics*	
1797	Hölderlin, *Hyperion* Schelling, *Philosophy of Nature* Heine, Schubert born	
1798	Schiller, *Wallenstein* trilogy first performed in Weimar Wordsworth and Coleridge, *Lyrical Ballads*	French troops occupy Rome Napoleon in Egypt Battle of the Nile
1799	Novalis, *Christendom, or Europe*	Second coalition against France Napoleon becomes First Consul
1800	Schelling, *System of Transcendental Idealism* Schiller, *Mary Stuart*	
1801	Schiller, *The Maid of Orleans* Novalis dies	
1802	Dumas, Hugo born	Peace of Amiens
1803	Schiller, *The Bride of Messina* Herder dies Klopstock dies	
1804	Schiller, *William Tell* Kant dies	Napoleon crowned Emperor
1805	Schiller dies	Third coalition against France Battles of Trafalgar and Austerlitz
1806	Arnim and Brentano, *The Boy's Magic Horn*, vol. 1 (dedicated to Goethe)	Battle of Jena/Auerstedt Capitulation of Prussia Holy Roman Empire ceases to exist

Year	*Life*
1807	Duchess Anna Amalia, mother of Duke Karl August, dies
1808	Publication of *Faust I*
	Meets Napoleon at Erfurt
1809	*The Elective Affinities*
	Pandora
1810	*Theory of Colour*
1811	*Poetry and Truth* (to 1814)
1812	Meets Beethoven in Teplitz
1814	Starts poems in the manner of Hafiz
1816	*Italian Journey* (to 1817)
	Christiane dies
1819	*West-Eastern Divan*
1821	*Wilhelm Meister's Journeyman Years*
1828	Duke Karl August dies
1829	First public performance of *Faust I*, in Braunschweig
1830	Goethe's only surviving child, August, dies in Rome
	Chinese-German Days and Seasons
1832	Goethe dies on 22 March
	Faust II published

Year	Cultural Context	Historical Context
1807	Hegel, *Phenomenology of Mind*	Peace of Tilsit
1809	Darwin born	
1811	Kleist dies	
1812	Grimm, *Fairy Tales*	Napoleon's Russian campaign
	J. von Hammer's translation of Hafiz' *Divan* (to 1814)	
1813	Wieland dies	
	Verdi and Wagner born	
1814		Napoleon exiled to Elba
1815		The Hundred Days
		Battle of Waterloo
1816	Clausewitz, *On War*	
	Rossini, *The Barber of Seville*	
1817	Byron, *Manfred*	
1819	Schopenhauer, *The World as Will and Imagination*	
	Mary Ann Evans (George Eliot) born	
1821		Greek uprising against Turkish rule
1824	Byron dies	
1825	Manzoni, *The Betrothed*	
1827	Heine, *Book of Songs*	
1831	Hegel dies	

Introduction

The claim that Goethe is a modern classic ought not to be controversial. *Faust* should stand alongside *Hamlet*, *The Divine Comedy*, and *War and Peace* – and so, in continental Europe at any rate, it does. Britain has been less sure. The Victorians accused Goethe of irreligion and immorality in sexual and marital matters. Twentieth-century Britain, victorious in two World Wars, believed in its moral and cultural superiority over the (allegedly) humourless, metaphysical, and alarmingly thorough Germans. But insofar as it has any grounds, the British incomprehension of Goethe's status originates from the nature of the claims that are made for his historical significance. From a British perspective, Goethe is a Romantic writer; he is the writer of delicate or tempestuous lyrics set to music by Schubert and others (e.g. 'Prometheus', p. 12), the writer of the epic drama *Faust* about the solitary striving of man. On this basis, grand claims for his historical significance would of course sound far-fetched. Lumbered with the label Romantic, Goethe is associated with the lack of breadth and the built-in obsolescence which, to British minds, Romanticism implies.

Goethe's writing career spanned eight decades, from the 1760s, when Johnson and Voltaire were still alive, to 1832, when Mary Ann Evans was a teenager and soon to become George Eliot. Although this career overlapped with Romanticism, Goethe never thought of himself as a Romantic. His career began in the Enlightenment, and one of his achievements was to bring together elements of the Enlightenment and Romanticism. He was, one might say, the only major European writer to transcend the literary fashions of the time. His alternative to Romanticism was a form of neo-Classicism. With classical poets as his models – principally Homer, the Greek lyricist Pindar, the tragedian Euripides, and the Roman elegiac poets – Goethe created a form in which to express his own personal experience (in that sense he was a Romantic) but which also stood for the universal human values of the Enlightenment.

Goethe also avoided the Romantic tendency to specialise. He was the last of the true polymaths, expert in a whole range of learned and practical disciplines: literature, the visual arts, natural science, politics, the law, education. He also defied the trend of specialisation in literature, writing in all genres. There is no other writer of that time or since who has produced work of the very highest class, as Goethe did, in lyric and narrative poetry, in verse and prose drama, in the long serial novel and the short story. Fittingly, *Faust*, his life's work and the work for which he is known best, is a hybrid – a drama, which like a novel narrates the life of a modern individual, but which tells it in an allusive and poetic form.

The confidence to aim for such breadth came from Goethe's family and the city of Frankfurt where he grew up. Goethe was virtually alone among the major German writers of the later eighteenth-century in not either training as a Protestant pastor or having a father who was one. His family was a combination of the *nouveau riche* mercantile (on his father's side) and the professional and administrative patrician classes (on his mother's). The Imperial Free City of Frankfurt was self-governing. It thus suffered fewer of the social and political constraints which held back most of the 360-odd constituent statelets of the 'Holy Roman Empire of the German Nation'. Although technically the Goethes were bourgeois and were thus excluded from high rank in the military or administrative service of the Holy Roman Empire and most of its principalities, *de facto* they were part of the local aristocracy, in a city which had little real aristocracy to speak of.

Frankfurt was a charmed world in which to grow up for an eighteenth-century German poet, but also an unrepresentative one. Elsewhere in Germany, any of Goethe's contemporaries who wanted to make writing their living faced an uphill struggle and bitter disappointments. The lack of a copyright law meant that the financial rewards of literary success were very short-lived. A best-seller might be pirated within weeks of its publication, and as the pirate publisher had no author's royalties or advance to pay, he could undercut the original edition. So even a successful writer had to have a day-job. For respectability's sake this meant the church or teaching (government and the military were the preserves of the nobility), and it required a training, which had to be paid for. Payment might come in the form of a grant from an aristocratic patron, often in turn entailing a commitment to a career in the church. (Aristocratic patronage of the arts was strong in eighteenth-century Germany, but it tended to benefit musicians more than writers; a stable and productive career such as Haydn's at the court of the Esterházys was inconceivable for a writer.) Possibilities for escape from this servitude were an academic career, poorly paid and hard to come by, or the isolated and depressing life of a private tutor to a wealthy family. His family wealth and the independent traditions of Frankfurt meant that Goethe could avoid all of this. They also gave him a sense that he deserved social recognition and the ambition and confidence to demand it.

His unusual social background shaped Goethe's literary career from beginning to end. Political events also played their part. For most of the eighteenth century Europe was relatively peaceful, although dynastic complications did give rise to a few small-scale wars. The last of these, the Seven Years' War (1756–63), threatened to drag Germany back into the mayhem of the previous century, when the Thirty Years' War (1618–48) had devastated large parts of Germany and set back the development of German culture. Goethe's career as a writer began in the aftermath of the Seven Years' War, which was marked by an uneasy stand-off between the two chief combatants and largest German states, Austria and Prussia, each seeking to extend its sphere of influence among the smaller German states ('Austro–Prussian dualism'). This atmosphere encouraged 'cultural nationalism' among the German intelligentsia, the attempt to create a linguistic and cultural German identity in the absence of a political one. It sought to promote the unity of the German states through their common language and culture. In Lessing's comedy *Minna von Barnhelm*, the Prussian hero and Saxon heroine overcome their mutual incomprehension and are finally united in love. (The Seven Years' War had begun with Prussia's invasion of Saxony.) Promoting indigenous German culture was itself a political statement. In doing so the cultural nationalists defied the claims of the Francophile Prussian capital Berlin and the Italophile Austrian capital Vienna to lead German cultural life.

In the early 1770s Goethe and his friend Johann Gottfried Herder, philosopher and cultural critic (1744–1803), formed the nucleus of a literary movement that came to be known as 'Sturm und Drang' (Storm and Stress). Storm and Stress was a protest at the condition of Germany under Austro–Prussian dualism. Its main target was the imported culture of Berlin and Vienna. It borrowed its central ideas from the philosopher Jean-Jacques Rousseau's (1712–78) critique of the idea of progress and his advocacy of primitivism and a 'return to nature'. The main literary inspiration of Storm and Stress was Shakespeare; the movement was part of a wider Anglophile trend in 1770s Germany, in opposition to the Latinate culture of the leading courts and cities. Goethe's historical drama *Götz von Berlichingen* tells the story, in Shakespearian style, of a rough-hewn fifteenth-century independent Imperial Knight who is destroyed by his greedy larger neighbours, thus indicating the fate that threatened Frankfurt and the other small German states.

In 1775 Goethe turned his back on Frankfurt and the Storm and Stress movement, taking up a position as companion to the young Duke Karl August of Sachsen-Weimar. His work in Weimar, where he lived for the rest of his life, at first continued the project of cultural nationalism. Unlike Frankfurt, Weimar had no distinct political or cultural profile. Part of the attraction of this small, poor territory strategically located between the Prussian and Austrian spheres of influence was that it was a blank page. The Duke's mother Anna Amalia had attracted the poet and novelist Christoph Martin Wieland (1733–1813) to Weimar, and soon after his own arrival Goethe persuaded the Duke to employ Herder. With Goethe and Herder on board, the Weimar 'court of the Muses' set out to offer a new alternative to the dual dominance of Prussia and Austria. Instead of culture in the Anglophile, primitivistic mode of Storm and Stress, this was a culture in the classical style, more suited to a German court with political aspirations and diplomatic needs. This shift to a more 'establishment' form of culture did not worry Goethe. A taste for the classical was what any respectable bourgeois would want to cultivate. (The same was true in late eighteenth-century England: classicism was by no means a sign of social conservatism.) Goethe still attempted to steer away from the Gallic culture of Prussia, to which the Duke was inclined. Besides continuing to write in the Storm and Stress forms of simple song and ballad, he developed a new form of 'naturalistic' classicism, quite different from classicism in the French style. The drama *Iphigenia at Tauris* is classicism in a naturalistic style; its first version (1779) was written in a relatively informal prose which falls naturally into iambic rhythms. Goethe's classical-inspired lyrics of this period are in a similarly idiomatic free verse, even if they use a spikier syntax to convey their admonitions against aristocratic complacency ('Winter Journey in the Harz', 'The Divine').

In 1789 the French Revolution changed the political landscape altogether and made Goethe's cultural balancing act still more difficult. Most German intellectuals supported the Revolution at first, but in the gathering chaos began to change their allegiance. The execution of Louis XVI in January 1793 finally made support for the Revolution impossible for all but the few diehard German Jacobins. By this stage Weimar was formally allied with Prussia. Duke Karl August commanded a regiment of Prussian cavalry in the campaigns against the revolutionary armies in 1792 and 1793. Throughout this period Goethe tried to remain impartial. He was unusual in that he was suspicious about the Revolution from the start. That is not to say that he was a natural ally of the royalist, anti-Revolutionary party, for he was careful to show his distaste for them too (despite having been ennobled himself in 1782).

From 1794 Goethe joined with the dramatist Friedrich Schiller (1749–1805) in a two-man campaign to reform German culture. The aesthetic ideal which Goethe and Schiller promoted was a continuation of Goethe's naturalistic classicism of the 1780s. The 'Roman Elegies' (pp. 36–41), published in 1794, were the epitome of this style, urbane and passionate, simple and educated: in short, balanced between the poles of German literary culture, as Goethe saw it. In the decade after the Revolution, public life in Germany became increasingly polarised between those who thought that moderate and gradual reforms would help Germany to avoid France's fate and those who wanted to return to the Old Regime and eradicate all traces of the Revolution. Instead of siding with one party, Goethe and Schiller made enemies of both. The philosopher Johann Gottlieb Fichte (1762–1814) – soon to be dismissed from his chair at Jena on a charge of atheism in the increasingly sensitive political atmosphere – summed up Goethe's position between court and bourgeoisie: 'You want to divide yourself between the two and so you end up, between two such hard task-masters, in the unenviable position of pleasing neither.'

The series of alliances against France and Napoleon's occupation of large parts of Europe in the first decade of the nineteenth century brought previously unimaginable changes to the German lands, including in 1806 the dissolution of the Holy Roman Empire. Goethe's attitude towards Napoleon was unusual. He saw in

Napoleon not Germany's conqueror, but an end to the Revolution and, consequently, the possibility of a new, durable order in Europe. Above all he admired Napoleon's personality and the 'daemonic' force which seemed to reside in him. Goethe's writing of this period reflects this sense of personal power and destiny and of the fragility of civilisation before the force of the 'daemonic'. At the same time Goethe turned increasingly away from German literary and political affairs and outwards towards the rest of Europe. As modern Europe's first literary superstar, he saw a constant flow of visitors in Weimar and built a wide network of contacts across Europe. He rejected attempts to enlist him for the nationalist campaign to 'liberate' Germany following Napoleon's Russian debacle. After the Restoration, in the new and oppressive atmosphere of post-Napoleonic Germany, he became increasingly sceptical about the idea even of German cultural nationalism, preferring to focus on what he called 'Weltliteratur' (world-literature) and to sustain his literary and scientific contacts in Britain, France, Italy and elsewhere. He welcomed comment on his work from abroad, and was particularly pleased by reviews of the third Act of *Faust II* which appeared in Moscow, Paris, and Edinburgh in 1827 and 1828. On finishing *Faust II* in 1831 he sealed and locked away his bequest to the Germans for posthumous publication, an ironic comment on the reaction he expected from his German readers.

Goethe's place in the history of European culture is central, but unusually so. He tended to take strongly against dominant features of his world, as if they were a personal challenge to him. In a sense this was the eighteenth-century fashion for melancholy writ large. Goethe was notoriously touchy and a great harbourer of injured feelings. He spent twenty years engaged in a bitter and largely pointless campaign against Newton's theory of light. The real issue was not the scientific truth or otherwise of Newton's theory, except in the sense that Newton's authority, buttressed by the scientific establishment, only made Goethe more determined to disprove him. What really mattered was that Goethe felt something that he had experienced himself – the integrity of white light and the presence of colours only on the margins of light and dark – was being denied. He felt that his experience compelled him to object. Matthew Arnold summed up the significance of Goethe as well as anyone: 'Goethe's profound, imperturbable naturalism was absolutely fatal to all routine thinking; he puts the standard, once for all, inside every man instead of outside him.' In that sense Goethe was the pre-eminent voice of the Enlightenment, of the ideal that everyone has the right to challenge authority, that truth is defined as personal experience brought into the public arena, that the goal of life is fullness of experience and of the possession of truth. One of the characteristics of Romanticism was its retreat from the Enlightenment's marriage of truth to personal fulfilment. There is something of this Romantic retreat in the lines on Goethe in Arnold's 'Memorial Verses': 'And he was happy, if to know / Causes of things . . . be happiness.' The summary is, nonetheless, entirely apt.

MATTHEW BELL

Note on the Translations

This selection of Goethe's poems aims to give an English-speaking audience a brief chronological overview of the work of Germany's greatest lyric poet. From the massive volume of his output it can illustrate only a part of the wide range of his themes and their variety of metrical forms. Particular importance is attached to replicating in English Goethe's metrical and rhyming patterns as far as possible in the hope that this would help to convey some idea of the sound and flavour of his poetry along with its sense.

Goethe

May Song (March 1771)

How splendid nature
Shines all for me!
The sun, it sparkles!
Fields laugh with glee!

From all the branches 5
The blossoms push,
A thousand voices
From every bush

And joy and rapture
From every breast. 10
O earth, o sunshine,
O bliss, o zest,

O love, o love,
So golden bright
As clouds of morning 15
Upon that height,

On fresh fields richly
Your blessings spill,
With haze of blossom
The world you fill! 20

O girl my darling
How I love you!
Your eyes, how shining!
How you love too!

So loves the skylark 25
Its song on high
And morning flowers
The fragrant sky

As I am burning
With love for you 30
Who give me courage
And youth anew,

Give joy, set singing
And dancing free;
Be ever happy 35
As you love me.

Meeting and Parting (Spring 1771)

My heart beat wild. And off, like lightning!
I rode as if to meet the foe.
In evening cradled earth was quietening
And on the hills the night hung low.
In cloak of mist the oak tree towered, 5
Rearing like a giant there
Where darkness from the bushes glowered
With all a hundred eyes' black stare.

On high-banked clouds the moon was peering
From out the haze with sleepy eyes, 10
The winds on quiet wings were veering
And passed me by with awesome sighs.
Though night spawned monstrous thousands lowering
A thousandfold more bold I stood,
My spirit was a flame devouring 15
And all my heart a burning flood.

I saw you, and the gentling sweetness
Flowed over me with each look from you.
Whole was my heart, you brought completeness,
For you was every breath I drew. 20
A rosy hue of springtime's season
Coloured that dearest lovely face

And tenderness for me, beyond reason,
Ye gods, I'd hoped, not earned, such grace.

The parting, how oppressed, how troubled! 25
Your looks spoke all your heart again.
In all your kisses love redoubled!
How great the bliss, how great the pain!
You went, downcast I stood unmoving
And followed you with moistening eyes. 30
And yet, what prize to win such loving,
To love, oh gods, oh what a prize!

Mohammed's Song (1772–3)

See the spring in the cliff
Bright with joy
Like the radiance of stars!
Over clouds
Its youth was nurtured 5
By good spirits
In the cliffs and scrub.

Youthful freshly
It dances from the cloud
Down to the marble cliffs below, 10
Jubilating
To the heavens.

Through the summit passes
It chases after the bright pebbles
And it strides as a young leader 15
Pulling its brother wellsprings
Along with it.

Down in the valley
Flowers come where it steps,

And the meadow 20
Lives from its breath.

But no shadowed valley can keep him,
Nor no flowers
Winding around his knees,
Flattering him with the eyes of love; 25
To the plain his course drives on,
Snakelike sliding.

Brooks sidle
Companionly.
Now he steps 30
On the plain resplendently silvered,
And the plain's resplendent with him,
And the rivers from the lowlands
And the brooklets from the mountains
Jubilate and cry out; brother, 35
Brother, take your brothers with you,
To your age-old father,
To the eternal ocean
Where with outspread arms
It awaits us; 40
Arms, alas, which open vainly
For the ones who're yearning for him;
For we're devoured in the barren desert
By greedy sand,

The sun up there 45
Sucks our blood,
A hillside
Hems us in as a pond.
Brother,
Take your brothers from the plains, 50
Take your brothers from the mountains
With you, with you to your father!

Come now all of you! –
And he swells up
More resplendent, all a tribe 55

Carries a prince aloft,
And rolling in triumph
He gives name to countries, cities
Spring up from his footsteps.

On he rushes irresistible, 60
Leaves the towers of flame-topped summits,
Marble houses, all created
By his abundance, all he leaves.

Cedar houses Atlas carries
On his giant shoulders, rippling 65
Sails that stream high up above him
Form a thousand confirmations
Of his power and his splendour.

Thus he carries all his brothers,
All his treasures and his children, 70
Foaming joyfully to the waiting
Heart of their progenitor.

Satyros
or
The Idolised Demon of the Woods[1]

(Autumn 1773)

from Act One

HERMIT. You think, dear Sirs, I've stepped aside
As life in towns I can't abide.
You're wrong though, all your guesses wide!
I didn't come here to the rabbits
Because the towns have shameful habits 5
And everyone by impulse plays
In false and fawning thievish ways:
All that had quite amusing seemed

Had they not sought to be esteemed,
To rob and shit on me undaunted, 10
And bows and scrapes as well they wanted!
Their tiresome clowning made me spew,
So here to God's City I withdrew;
Here too there's lots of rough and tumble
But nevertheless this one won't crumble. 15
I saw in spring the countless fill
Of buds and blooms through vale and hill,
How all's a thrusting driving need,
No peck of earth without its seed.
Then thinks the wooden Philistine: 20
All that is there for me and mine.
How kind today is God our Father;
In cupboard and barn it should be rather!
Our Lord God speaks: Not so, not true;
There's others who need to enjoy it too. 25
Then come enticed when sunshine starts
Storks and swallow from foreign parts,
From out its house the butterfly,
The flies from cracks wherein they lie,
And all the little larvae hatch out dry. 30
All that swells with the urge to beget
When it's freed itself from its sleepy net;
Midges, beasts, birds, frogs a-jumping,
Indulge every moment, bumping and thumping,
Backside and front, bellying and rumping, 35
So every flower and leaf they tread
Is a bridal and confinement bed.
And then my heart leaps up and sings
Praise God with worms and little things.
The crowd then wants to eat and be sated, 40
Devour the gifts by God donated.
So wormlet eats fresh leafy bud,
On wormlet lark feels full and good,
And as I too have an eating part
The little lark I take to heart. 45
For I'm a really domestic man,
Keep house, stable, garden as well as I can.
My garden, my fruit I guard as meet

From cold, from crawlers, from drought and heat.
But if the hailstones come my way 50
And forage my stuff away in a day
I grant their trick makes me tear my hair;
But when each year ends I'm still there
Though many a werewolf's already dead
Because it suffered hunger's dread. 55

from Act Four

SATYROS. Get ready for the journey deep and long
To gain all knowledge, listen to my song!
Hear, how the Non-Thing 290
Had everything confused in a turmoiled ring,
In their pent-up hatred elements out-welling,
And force against forces each other repelling,
No foe joining, no friend joining,
Neither destroying, nor increasing! 295
PEOPLE. Teach us, your lesson's pleasing!
SATRYOS. Hear, from the Non-Thing the Prime-Thing sprang out,
Through the night light's power rang out
Piercing all beings' depths with fire,
So germinated torrential desire 300
And the elements all exploded
In spate to mix by their hunger goaded,
All-penetrating, all penetrated.
HERMES. This man's spirit by gods was generated.
SATYROS. Hear, the birth of love and hate 305
Did from the All a Whole create,
And the Whole did resound
In living harmony working all round,
And force went at force in feeding,
And force went at force in breeding, 310
And up and down it rolled its ring,
That all and one and lasting Thing,
Forever changing, forever persisting!

Ganymede (Spring 1774)

How in the morning dawn
You glow all round me,
Springtime, beloved!
With love's blisses a-thousandfold
The sacred feeling 5
Of your eternal warmth
Pushes to my heart,
Infinite lovely one!

Could I but grasp you
Within this arm! 10

Oh, on your breast
I lie, languish,
And your flowers, your grass,
Thrust themselves at my heart.
You cool the burning 15
Thirst of my bosom,
Lovely breeze of the morning,
Through it the nightingale calls
Lovingly for me from the misty valley.

I come! I come! 20
To where? Oh, to where?

Upwards, upwards the urge,
The clouds are floating
Downwards, the clouds
Lower themselves towards yearning love, 25
To me, me!
In your lap
Upwards,
Embracing embraced!
Upwards 30
Upon your breast,
All-loving father!

The New Amadis[2] (1774)

As a boy they locked me in,
Years spent on my own,
So I sat with time to spin
With myself alone
Just as in the womb. 5

But you helped and filled my room,
Golden fantasy,
And I had a hero's rage
Like the Prince Pipi,
All the world my stage. 10

Crystal castles I would build
And destroy them too,
Dragons' blood my fierce thrusts spilled,
Pierced their entrails through,
Yes, I was a man! 15

Then I freed, as true knights can,
Princess Fish of fable;
She was more than *obligeant*,
Led me to her table,
And I was *galant*. 20

And her kiss was Heaven's bread,
Glowing like the wine,
Oh! I loved till nearly dead
Whilst round her the sun did shine
Painted in gold leaf. 25

Oh, who took her, who the thief?
Could no magic band
Her false flight gainsay?
Tell me, where now is her land,
How to find the way? 30

Prometheus (Autumn 1774)

Go cover up your heaven, Zeus,
With cloudy haze!
And practise, like some boy
Topping thistle-heads,
Your strength on oaks and mountain peaks! 5
Still you must leave standing
This my earth,
And my shelter
Which you did not build,
And this my hearth 10
Whose glowing heat you envy me.

There's nothing more pitiful
Under the sun than you gods.
You feed your majesty
With meagre victuals 15
Of sacrifices
And vaporous prayer,
And would be starving were not
Children and beggars
Credulous simpletons. 20

When I was a child,
Didn't know which way to go,
My bewildered eye turned
To the sun, as if up there were
An ear to hear my lamentations, 25
A heart like mine
With mercy to comfort the afflicted.

Who helped me counter
The Titans' arrogance?
From death who was it rescued me, 30
From slavery?
Was it not you that accomplished all,
Heart in sacred glow?

And yet glowed, young and good,
Deluded, with gratitude 35
To that sleeping one up there?

I honour you? For what?
Did you just once ease the torments
Of him who was burdened?
Did you just once still the weeping 40
Of him who was anguished?
Was not I made a man on the anvil
Of all-powerful time
And of fate everlasting,
My masters and yours? 45

Did you imagine
Perhaps I would hate existence,
Run off to deserts,
If not all my boyhood morning's
Blossom-dreaming fruited? 50

Here I sit, fashion humans
In my own image,
A breed to be my equal,
To suffer, sorrow,
To enjoy and be joyful, 55
And to ignore you,
Like me.

[Untitled – from *Egmont*][3] (1774–5)

Glad heart
And sad heart,
And weighed down with thought,
Nearing
And fearing 5
In torment still caught,

Shouting the skies out,
Now ready to die,
Happy alone
Is the heart on love's high. 10

New Love, New Life (Early 1775)

Heart, my heart, what are you doing?
What's oppressing you so sore?
Strange, this new life you're pursuing –
I don't know you any more.
Gone is all you loved, all gladness, 5
Gone now all that troubling sadness,
Diligence, and rest, all gone –
Oh, what was it brought this on?

Are you gripped by youth all flowering?
By this lovely form's amaze, 10
By the endless overpowering
Of this kind and faithful gaze?
If I say that I'll not see her,
Steel myself and try to flee her,
Instantly I'm on a track – 15
Oh – that simply leads me back.

On this thread that nothing severs,
Magic spun with magic skill,
This girl, winsome-wilful, tethers
Me so much against my will: 20
In her magic circle's passions
My life now she rules and fashions.
Oh, the change, how great a blow!
Love, oh love, oh let me go!

Lili's Park (1775)

There's no other menagerie
Like my Lili's ownest!
The strangest creatures she traps all alonest
And no one knows how, not even she.
With wings clipped back o how they flutter, 5
O how they jump and run and scutter,
The poor poor princes, what a rout,
In pangs of love they can't dowse out!

'Her name, this sorceress? Lili?' – Don't ask again!
If you don't know, thank God who kept you sane. 10

O what a noise, o what a cackle,
When in the doorway at last she comes
And holds in her hands the basket of crumbs!
O all the squeals, o all the quackle!
All the trees and all the bushes 15
Seem to become animated:
Whole hordes of them agitated
Rush to her feet, and each impatient fish pushes
It's head from the *bassin* and splashes in and out;
And then she strews the feed about 20
With such a look – the gods befopping,
Let alone the creatures. And then starts the chopping
And the slurping and the pecking;
They're higgledy-piggledy neck and necking,
Shove themselves, crush themselves, fight themselves, 25
Chase themselves, fright themselves, bite themselves,
And all that for a crust of bread
That, bone-dry, from those lovely finger tips
Has all the taste of ambrosial sips.

But then that look, and that tone 30
When she cries: Tweetwee! Tweetwee!
Jupiter's eagle she'd pull from his throne;
And Venus' doves twain,

Even the peacock so vain,
I swear they'd come ruffled 35
If they heard that tone even far off and muffled.

Just so in the forest's night she caught
One big bear, unpolished and no breeding,
Mastered him by sheer misleading,
Him to her tame entourage she brought 40
And with the others tamed and taught –
Of course with a certain point excepted!
How lovely o! how good
She seemed to be! All of my blood
I would have given to water her flowers. 45

'But you said: I! Who? Why?'
Right then, gentlemen, straight: The bear am I!
Enmeshed in a filmy lacework therefore,
And at her feet on silky thread thus tethered.
But all about the how and wherefore 50
I'll tell you at some other stage;
Today I'm in too big a rage.

For oh! in one of my corner places
I stand and hear the distant natter,
See the far off flitter-flatter, 55
Turn round and scowl
And growl
And run off backwards just a few paces
And look round and scowl
And growl 60
And run again a few more paces
And yet at last I return to the fowl.

Then suddenly mad rage is starting,
A mighty spirit snorts nose-smarting,
Now wilds in me the inner bear. 65
What, you a fool, a simple hare!
Such a Tweetwee! A nut-cracking squirrel that idles!
My bristly neck rears up and bridles,
Unwonted service shocks.

And every little well-trained tree looks and mocks 70
At me! I rush from the bowling green,
From those sleek lawns that irritate me.
The box-tree cocks a snook to bait me!
I seek dark undergrowth, seek not to be seen,
Try to break through the hedges 75
And jump the fence round the edges.
But climbing and jumping all misfire,
A leaden spell now strikes me,
A spell that hooks and spikes me,
I writhe and toil, and then when I tire 80
I lie in cascading fountain jets
And gnash and wail till I'm nearly gone
But oh! my torment's heard by none
Save porcelain Oread statuettes.

Suddenly! oh, a sheer 85
Sense of bliss pierces every limb and member:
It's she who sings in the arbour here,
I hear that dear, dear voice that I remember,
The air is all warm, a flowering ecstasy,
Oh, perhaps her song is meant for me? 90

I press towards it, trampling shrubs I meet,
The bushes rush away, the trees retreat,
And so – again the creature lies at her feet.

She looks at it: 'A monster! but waggy!
For a bear too mild, 95
For a poodle too wild:
So shambly, knobbly, shaggy!'
His back with her neat little foot she tickles;
He thinks that he's in Paradise.
How each of his seven senses prickles! 100
And she – looks on with clear calm eyes.
I kiss her shoes, I chew the soles shyly,
Quite decently really for only a bear;
Cautiously I rise and snuggle inching slyly
Up to her knee – if the day's set fair 105
She lets it happen and scratches my furry

Ears and heftily pats my hair –
New-born in bliss I growl all purry.
Then her sweet empty mockery puts me on the spot:
'*Allons tout doux! eh la menotte!* 110
Et faites Serviteur,
Comme un joli Seigneur.'
So she carries on in play and laughter!
The oft duped dope has hope once more
But if he gets a little forward after 115
She keeps him short just like before.

But she's also got a balsam-fire,
Unlike this earth's honey, just a little phial,
And sometimes when she's softened by love and loyalty a
while
On the parched lips of her monster about to expire 120
Her finger strokes a droplet to reconcile,
And again she's off and leaves me to stew;
And I, liberated, am anew
Enspelled, am pulled to see her,
I seek her, shudder, again I flee her – 125
Thus she treats this wretch destroyed so sore,
If he's happy, or hurt, no word from her;
O yes, often she does half-open the door,
Glances mocking to see if escape's what I prefer.

And I! – Ye gods, if you have power to sunder 130
This stupefying magic spell I'm under
How I'll thank you if you set me free!
But if you won't help me now in good season –
Don't think I stretch these limbs without a reason:
I feel it! I swear it! I've still got strength in me. 135

On the Lake (June 1775)

(Later Version)

And now I suck fresh food, new blood,
From all the world with zest;
Dear nature, how she's fair and good
Who holds me to her breast!
The rocking wave lifts up our boat 5
In rhythm of the oars,
And mountains cloudy skywards float
To cut across our course.

Eyes, my eyes, why are you closing?
Golden dreams, once more proposing? 10
Dream, begone, though gold you be:
Here too love and life I see.

Stars in thousands blinking
Float on waves passing by,
Downy mists are drinking 15
Distance towering high:
Morning wind wings gently
Round the shadow-filled bay,
Ripening fruit contently
Mirrors itself in the sway. 20

Autumn Feeling (Autumn 1775)

Green more juicy, you leaves,
On vines of this trellis,
Up to my window here.
And swell more compact,
Twin-grown berries, and ripen 5
Quicker and gleaming fuller.

You brood of the sun's maternal
Afterglance, you are fanned by
The gracious heaven's
Fertile abundance. 10
You're cooled by the moon's
Friendly enspelling breath,
And you are dewed, alas,
From out these eyes by
The ever enlivening love in 15
Tears swelling to fullness.

Why give us deep vision . . . ? (April 1776)

Why give us deep vision so far-sighted
That foreboding we our future see,
That by love and earthly joys delighted
We cannot in bliss deluded be?
Why for us, fate, did you by this feeling 5
Bring our hearts into each other's scope,
So our true relationship revealing
As through explorations strange we grope?

Oh, so many thousand men drift feckless,
Sluggish-sensed, and hardly know their hearts, 10
Hover purposeless and then rush reckless
Through the pain of hopeless fits and starts;
Shout for joy again when darting pleasure
Unexpected dawns all rosy-eyed.
Just to us poor lovers is the treasure 15
Of that mutual happiness denied:
As we never were, to see each other,
Each to love yet not the other know,
Chase the happiness our dreams discover
And in peril-dreams sway to and fro. 20

Bliss, absorbed in empty dream's romances!
Bliss, foreboding brushed aside as wrong!
Sadly all the present, all our glances,
Make foreboding and our dream more strong.
Tell me, what is fate for us preparing? 25
Tell me, how it made us fit so true?
Oh, in some past life that we were sharing
You as sister or my wife I knew;

You knew every aspect of my being,
Noted how my very nerves vibrate, 30
Read me with one single glance far-seeing,
Me whom mortal eyes can't penetrate.
You dosed fevered blood with moderation,
Rectified the errant course run wild,
And the ravaged heart found restoration, 35
In your angel arms was reconciled;
Held him lightly bound in magic tether
Conjuring away the idling day.
Where's the bliss to match those hours together
When so grateful at your feet he lay, 40
Felt against your heart his heart grow lighter,
Saw himself in your eyes and felt good,
All his senses quickening and brighter
And a calming in his seething blood.

And from all of that alone the faltering 45
Memories round the unsure heart remain
While the former truth within still stays unaltering,
And its new condition turns to pain.
We feel we are only half existing,
Twilight dims for us the brightest day. 50
Glad that fate on torment is insisting
Yet won't alter us in any way.

Love Without Peace (May 1776)

'Gainst snow, 'gainst raining,
'Gainst head wind straining,
In chasms seething,
Through haze-mists wreathing,
Always on! always on! 5
No rest, peace all gone!

Better be sharing
Suffering and sadness
Rather than bearing
A life of such gladness. 10
All that attraction
Of heart to heart tending,
Strange, how its action
Makes pain unending!

How to get free now? 15
Forestwards flee now?
Vain, all such scheming!
Life's crown all gleaming,
Restlessness too,
Love, that is you! 20

To the Spirit of Johannes Secundus[4]

(November 1776)

Kind, and holy, famed for kisses,
You who so nearly pre-charted me
In my breathing thirsting ecstasy!
To whom should I lament if not to you!
You, whose poems were a heart's-ease to me, 5
Supporting me like a warming pillow of healing herbs,

So that once again from these earthly spasms
My heart recovered to beat once more.
Oh, how to tell you that my lip is bleeding,
That it's split and hurts so pitiable painful, 10
This lip of mine that is so accustomed
To swell with love's sweet happiness
And, like a golden portal of heaven,
To take in and give out the tones of blissful delirium.
Yes, it is split! Not from the bite of my fair one 15
Who, in the all-embracing fullness of her loving,
Wants only more of me, and wants the whole of me
Entirely in her kisses, devouring, whatever she could!
Not split because my lips were desecrated
By profane airs after she had breathed on me. 20
Split, alas, because I, cold, desolate,
Was seized by autumn winds in the cutting frost.
And now there's the juice of grapes and the honey-bee's
juices,
Both together by my friendly fire on the hearth,
That's there to help me! In fact, it doesn't help: 25
For of love's healing poisonous balm
They've not got a single droplet between them.

Need for Love

(Later version of the preceding poem,
between 1776 and 1789)

Who will hear me? oh, to whom lament it?
He who heard it, would he feel my suffering?
Oh, this lip which knew so many moments
Taking pleasures as well as giving pleasures,
Has been split, and miserably it hurts me. 5
Don't imagine that its chafe and soreness
Came because my dear was too voracious,
Bit me as she graced me, wanting only
More securely to enjoy her lover:

No, this delicate lip is split and tender 10
Just because the winds and frost confront me
Joined in sharp and spiteful combination.

And now it seems that the vine as juice ennobled
With the juice of bees, together at my fireside,
Are joined to comfort me and give me easement. 15
Oh, what use is that unless love mixes
One single droplet of its soothing lotion?

Winter Journey in the Harz (December 1777)

To match the hawk,
Who on heavy clouds of morning
At rest with languid pinion
Seeks out his prize,
Soar now my song. 5

For a god has
Set for each his course
Predetermined
Which the fortunate
Swiftly runs to its 10
Joyful term;
But if misfortune
Has garrotted his heart
He chafes in vain at
The fatal thread's limit 15
That tethers like iron,
Loosed by shearing that's bitter
And only once.

To fearsome thickets
Fierce wild beasts repair, 20
And with the reed sparrows
Rich men have long since wandered
Off to their winter hide in swamps.

Easy, following the chariot
When Dame Fortune steers, 25
Just like the footfollower's ease
When the prince makes his entry
Over the road's new surface.

Over there though, who's that?
See, his path is lost in the scrub, 30
Hard on his footsteps
The bushes are closing,
The grass springs back again,
The wasteland devours him.

Oh, who will heal the tormented, 35
Him whose balm turned to poison
Drinking misanthropy
From the copious wells of love?
First despised, and now too a despiser,
He consumes unseen 40
His own value's core
In self-seeking that sates not.

If your psalter's compass,
All-loving Father, has tones
Which can open his hearing 45
Let them freshen his heart!
Open up his clouded eye
To see the thousand wellsprings
Close by him thirsting there in the desert!

You who have made joys in plenty, 50
To each an overflowing measure,
Bless now the friends of the hunt
On the trail of the beast
In spirited excess of youth's
Murderous gaiety, 55
Late avengers of evils
Which the peasant for ages
Vainly resists with bludgeons.

But to the lonely one bring
Your golden cloudwrapping, 60
Bind round with evergreen
Till the rose once again matures
The winter-drenched hair,
Oh Love, of your poet!

With your glimmering lantern 65
You light his way
Through the fords in the night,
Over treacherous footpaths
On barren terrain;
With your thousand colours of morning 70
Your laughter is in his heart;
With the acid-sharp storm
High you transport him aloft.
Winter torrents plunge from the cliff tops
To flood his anthems, 75
For an altar of grateful love
He looks to the much-dreaded summit's
Snow-enveloped very top
Which the awe of nations
Wreathed with gathering spirits. 80

You stand with breast impenetrable
Mysterious and evident
Over the astonished world
And look from clouds
On all its kingdoms and its glory 85
Still nourished by you from the veins of brothers
Standing beside you.

The Angler (1778)

The water streamed, the water swelled,
An angler sat there too
And calmly watched the rod he held,
Chilled to his heart all through.
And as he sits and as he listens 5
The waters part and surge
And where the troubled water glistens
He sees a nymph emerge.

She sang to him, she spoke to him:
'Why tempt my children so 10
With human hearts and tricks untrue
To warm air's fatal glow?
How little fish – oh if you knew –
Feel cosy here below
Just as you are you'd come down too 15
And health at last you'd know.

Is sun, is moon not freshened when
In water's ease they bathe?
Have they not twice more beauty then
From breathing ocean's wave? 20
Does this deep sky not pull you near,
This moist transfigured blue?
Does your own face not pull down here
To this eternal dew?'

The water streamed, the water swelled, 25
It wet his naked feet;
His heart by yearning was compelled
As when two lovers greet.
To him she spoke, to him she sang;
Resistance was in vain: 30
She half pulled him and half he sank,
And was not seen again.

Darling trees, do you need telling (1780)

Darling trees, do you need telling,
You I planted, half aware,
When those dawn-red dreams enspelling
Danced so wondrous in the air?
How I love, oh, you know surely, 5
Her who loves me answeringly
And who gives me back more purely
That most pure of drives in me.

From my heart, then, grow and flourish,
Thrust up striving in the air; 10
For your roots have soils that nourish,
Joy and pains I buried there.
Give me shade, give fruit's rich blessing,
Every day new joys confer:
Give, but let me then be pressing, 15
Pressing, pressing close to her!

Erl-king (1782)

Who rides so late through night so wild?
It is the father with his child;
He holds the boy firmly in his arm,
He keeps him warm and safe from harm.

Why hide your face, my son, why fear? – 5
The Erl-king, father, don't you see him here?
The Erl-king with his robe and crown? –
My son, it's mist that's drifting down. –

'You sweet child, come with me now, do!
Really lovely games I'll play with you; 10

By the water-side many bright flowers grow,
My mother has many gold robes to show.'

My father, my father, can you not hear
The Erl-king's promises whispered clear? –
Rest child, rest, it's only the trees 15
And the wind that's rustling through the dry leaves. –

'Would you like, fine boy, to come with me?
My daughters will care for you handsomely:
They dance the roundel when night is deep,
They'll rock you and dance you and sing you to sleep.' 20

My father, my father, don't you see, look there,
In that gloom the Erl-king's daughters fair? –
My son, my son, I see it right:
The old willow-trees look so grey at night.

'I love you, your fair form excites my delight; 25
If you struggle I'll force you with all my might.'
My father, my father, he's grabbing me more!
Erl-king's dragging has made me sore! –

The father shudders, he rides still more wild,
He holds in his arms his groaning child, 30
Reaches the farm through turmoil and dread;
In his arms the child was dead.

The Divine (1783)

Noble, let man be,
Helpful and good!
For that alone
Distinguishes him
From all beings 5
That we know of.

Hail to the unknown
Higher beings
Sensed in the mind!
Let man be as they are! 10
His example teach us
Belief in them.

For nature
Is unfeeling:
The sun's light shines 15
On the wicked and the good,
And transgressor and the best
Alike see the gleaming
Of the moon and the stars.

Wind and waters, 20
Thunder and hailstones
Roar on their course
And hurrying on
Seize as they go
One after the other. 25

So too fortune
Gropes among the crowd,
Grasping now the child's
Curly-haired innocence
Now too the balding 30
Head of the guilty.

By eternal, iron,
Mighty laws
Must each and all of us
Complete the circles 35
Of our existence.

Only man alone
Can do the impossible:
He can distinguish,
Chooses and judges; 40
He can endow
The moment with permanence.

He alone may
Reward the good man,
Punish the wicked, 45
Restore and rescue,
Usefully bind
All that errs and wanders.

And we venerate
The immortal ones, 50
As if they were humans,
And did on the grand scale
What the best in his small way
Does or would wish to.

Let the noble man 55
Be helpful and good!
Untiring let him do
The right and the useful,
And pre-figure for us
Those sensed higher beings. 60

Dedication (August 1784)

The morning came; it drove off sleep that held me
So tenderly in slumber as I lay
And wakening me, with soul refreshed, compelled me
To leave my hut and climb the mountain way;
At every step each new-sprung flower enspelled me 5
With joy to see its dew-filled sparkling play;
The young enraptured day rose up before me,
All quickened fresh to quicken and restore me.

And as I climbed there softly crept beside me,
In swathes from meadow stream, a mist close by, 10
Receding, changing, flowing round to hide me
And soaring overhead to fill the sky.

The lovely view's refreshment was denied me,
A sombre drape the prospect for my eye;
A sea of clouds around me undulated 15
And closed in twilight I stood isolated.

The sun seemed suddenly to be defeating
The mist and there appeared a clarity.
The mist here sank, in gentle fall retreating,
Or split round woods and peaks and rose up free. 20
O how I hoped to give that light my greeting!
After gloom, I hoped, twice lovelier it must be.
The aerial strife was nowhere near decision,
Then a radiance ringed me, blinding all my vision.

But soon my eyes were opening and clearing, 25
Some drive within my heart my spirit raised,
I only dared quick glances in that searing
Where seemingly all glowed and burned and blazed.
I saw a hovering cloud-borne image nearing
And on a woman's form divine I gazed, 30
In all my life I saw no form more lovely,
She looked at me and swayed a while above me.

'Don't you know me?' from lips the words were spoken
Whence flowed all love and loyalty's dear sound,
'Know me, who when life's wounding left you broken 35
For you so often purest balm have found?
You know me well, to whom your heart in token
Of union everlastingly was bound.
Did I not see you with your heart's tears burning
For me already in your boyhood yearning?' 40

'Yes!' I cried out, immediately kneeling
In whelming bliss, 'it's you I long have sensed:
You gave me peace, to my young limbs brought healing
When restless passion tossed and turned and tensed;
On my hot brow you laid a cooling feeling 45
As if by gentle heavenly plumes dispensed:
You gave me gifts the best of earthly treasure,
Through you alone I'll seek all joy and pleasure!

I name you not. By others less reflective
I hear you named, each claims you as his own, 50
Though every eye thinks you are its objective
To nearly all your light strikes pain unknown.
Ah, when I erred I had friends with like perspective,
Now that I know you I am near alone;
My joy must stay a lonely contemplation 55
With your fair light locked up in isolation.'

She smiled, then spoke: 'How needful, now you see,
How wise, to refrain from self-revelations!
Scarcely from crass delusion are you free,
Scarcely you've mastered childish inclinations, 60
You claim a superhuman's quality
And so neglect all manly obligations!
Are you so special, so to be lamented?
Now know yourself, live with the world contented!'

'Forgive', I cried, 'you know it was well-meant. 65
Shall I see aimlessly when you are guiding?
My blood runs quick with good and glad intent,
Your gifts I value for their worth abiding.
For others shall my nobler wealth be spent,
My talents cannot, shall not, stay in hiding! 70
Why did I yearn to find the way to go
If not to brothers afterwards to show?'

And as I spoke the look from that high being
Was solace and indulgence for my plight;
And in her eye myself entirely seeing 75
I knew where I had failed and where done right.
She smiled, I sensed the healing and the freeing,
My spirit rose to heights of new delight;
I neared her with deep trust and dedication,
From close nearby absorbed in contemplation. 80

And then she followed with her hand the swaying
Swathes of cloud that drifted here and there;
It let itself be gathered without fraying
And was no longer mist that clouds the air.

I stood, the valley once again surveying, 85
I saw the sky, it was sublimely fair.
And she, I saw, the purest veil was holding,
It flowed round her in myriad folds enfolding.

'I know you, know your weakness, your endeavour,
I know the good that lives and glows in you!' 90
Just so she spoke, I hear her words forever,
'Receive what I long marked out as your due!
The fortunate one knows deprivation never
Whose quiet soul accepts this gift anew:
From sunlight's clarity and scent of morning 95
By truth enwoven, poetry's veil adorning.

And when your friends and you look for some healing
From sultry noon, toss high this veil outspread!
An evening breeze, its cooling balm unsealing,
Shall breathe on you and flowers' essence shed. 100
Then shall subside all anxious earthly feeling,
The sombre vault become a cloudy bed,
The pounding waves of life be moderated,
The day grow sweet, the night illuminated!'

So come, my friends, when life for you seems blighted, 105
By burdens ever heavier oppressed,
Then when by flowers and golden fruits delighted
You find your path is once more newly blessed
To meet the next day we shall go united!
So we shall live, in happiness so quest. 110
And when our children mourn for us hereafter
Our love shall last to bring them joy and laughter.

To the Moon (1787–8)

(Later Version)

Filling wood and vale you cast
Quietly misty sheen,
And for once release at last
All my soul serene;

On my fields you spread your gaze 5
And alleviate,
As a dear friend's eye surveys
Gently all my fate.

Every glad and sad time's tone
My heart feels again, 10
I in solitude alone
Walk in joy and pain.

Dearest stream, flow on, flow on!
Joy I'll never know;
Just so jest and kiss are gone, 15
Faithfulness just so.

Once I really owned for sure
Sweetness haunting yet!
That we must the rack endure
Never to forget! 20

Downdale, stream, now rush along,
Restless ceaselessly
Rush, and whisper to my song
All your melody

When in winter you submerge 25
Night in raging floods,
Or in springtime when you surge
Round the bright young buds.

Bliss, to shut the world outside
Though no hate to bear, 30
And in one dear friend confide
And the pleasure share

That, by other men not known
Or not judged aright,
Roams the labyrinthine zone 35
Of the heart at night.

Roman Elegies (1788–90)

I

Tell me, stones, and call out, O speak, you lofty *palazzi!*
Streets, O talk to me now! Genius, will you not stir?
Yes, all is animate here within your sanctified ramparts,
Rome everlasting; from me only its voice is withheld.
O, who whispers to me, and where's the window that lets me 5
See that creature most fair whose fire shall freshen my life?
Have I not yet sensed those paths where I shall ever and ever,
Going and coming from her, squander the treasure of time?
Still I gaze at palace and church, at ruins and columns,
Serious-minded like one putting his tour to good use. 10
But soon all that is gone; then there'll be only one temple,
Amor's temple alone, where the initiate's received.
You indeed are a world, O Rome; but failing love's presence
World would not truly be world, nor then would Rome still be Rome.

III

Rue not, beloved, the haste that made you so swiftly surrender!
Trust me, I don't think you base, mine are not insolent thoughts.
So diverse are the arrows of Amor: some just make scratches,
And the poison that creeps sickens the heart year on year.
But with powerful pinions, and sharpened fresh from the whetstone, 5
Others will pierce to the quick, cunningly fire the blood.
In the heroic age, when goddess or god had a passion
Just one glance roused desire, straightway desire had its feast.
Think now, how long did love's goddess reflect and delay her decision
Seeing Anchises' fair form there in the Idaen grove? 10
And had Luna delayed to kiss the beautiful sleeper
Jealous Aurora for sure would quickly have kissed him awake.
Hero caught sight of Leander at the revels, and the lover
Hurled himself hot from the feast into the nocturnal tide.
Rhea Silvia, princess and virgin, wanders down to the Tiber 15
Meaning to draw some water, and there she's seized by the god.
Thus did Mars produce sons for himself! – The twin-born are suckled
By a she-wolf, and Rome calls herself Queen of the World.

V

Now on classical ground I'm happy to sense it inspires me;
Past and present speak louder, exciting me more.
Here I heed good advice, I leaf through the works of the ancients
With assiduous hand, daily delighting anew.

But when it comes to the nights I'm otherwise busied by Amor; 5
And if I'm only half-taught doubly I'm happy instead.
And don't I teach myself by watching the bosom's endearing
Forms that charm me, my hands gliding below down the hips?
Then I really know marble at last: I think in comparing,
See with the eye as it feels, feel with the hand as it sees. 10
Though my love may be stealing some of the hours from my daytime
She gives full compensation in the hours of night.
Not that it's kissing alone, there's also sensible talking;
When she's fallen asleep I will just lie and reflect.
Often too in her arms I lay and worked out a poem; 15
Counting hexameter's length, softly my fingering hand
Measured it out on her back. She breathes in the sweetest of slumbers,
And I am warmed by her breath glowing all through me within.
Amor trims up the lamp meanwhile and thinks of that era
When he performed that same task serving his Triumvirate.[5] 20

VII

O how happy my feelings in Rome! to think what I lived through,
Back there up North, when the days held me in greyness enclosed,
Skies sinking down on my head, sombre and heavily pressing,
Round me, exhausted, the world all without colour and form,
When I delved through my mind to trace in silent reflection 5
How my unappeased self floundered on darkening paths.
Now this ether-bright light illumines my brow with its radiance;

Forms and colours spring forth, summoned by Phoebus the god;
Night is starbright aglow, with song is gently melodious,
And the moon shines for me brighter than day in the North. 10
Me, a mortal, what bliss was given to me! Dreams? Am I now in
Your ambrosial house, Jupiter Father, your guest?
Ah, I lie here before you in supplication and raise my
Outstretched hands. Hear my plea, Jupiter Xenius, hear!
Really I can't explain it, the way I got here; but Hebe 15
Came to the wanderer and brought me here to enter your halls.
Did you give her the instruction to bring a hero as guest here?
Was she in error? Forgive! Let me keep error's reward!
And your daughter Fortuna, she too! a girl who disburses
Marvellous gifts by whim just as her fancy dictates. 20
Are you the god of all guests? O banish him not from Olympus,
Do not send back the guest once more to earth down below! –
'Poet! You climb too high from your place!' – Forgive me; the rising
Hill of the Capitol forms a second Olympus for you.
Jupiter, bear with me here, and let Hermes lead me hereafter 25
Down past Cestius's tomb gently to Orcus below.

XV

I would never have gone and marched after Caesar to Britain,
Florus would have easily dragged me away and off to the pub!
For the mists of the North are sad and by far the more hateful
Than the assiduous fleas swarming all over the South.
And I'll greet you more warmly from this day onwards, you taverns, 5
Osterie, as so aptly you're called here in Rome;

For you showed me my darling today, with her uncle beside her
Whom she often deceives so she can have me again.
Here our table stood, familiar with Germans around it;
There by her mother's seat, that's where the child found a place, 10
Often shifting the bench, with graceful manners contriving
That I saw half her face and the full view of her neck.
Louder than normal for Roman women she talked, raised the bottle,
Turned round and looked towards me, poured and the wine missed her glass.
Wine flowed over the board and she, with neat dainty finger, 15
Drew on the table's leaf circling lines from the wet.
My and her name she tangled together there; I kept my avid
Eyes on her finger's quick moves, and she observed that I did.
Nimbly ending she added a Five in the script of the Romans
And in front put a stroke. Quick, when I'd seen, she rubbed, 20
Winding circles through circles to blot out the letters and numbers;
But that most exquisite *Four* stayed as if stamped in my eyes.
I remained silent and sat there and bit my lip till it hurt me,
Half in pleasure and tease, half in the pangs of desire.
First the long wait until night! and then still four hours of waiting! 25
Sun resplendent, you pause, gazing a while on your Rome!
You have seen nothing more great and won't see anything greater,
As was foretold by your priest, Horace, in thrills of delight.
But today don't linger at all and cut short your looking,
Leave the sevenfold hills earlier and readier for once! 30

For the sake of a poet curtail the fine splendour of hours
  Painters enjoy with an eye raptured and greeding for
    more;
Let your last glowing look be quick to climb these facades
    now,
  Up over columns and domes and obelisks up and up;
Hurl yourself into the sea, to view the quicker tomorrow 35
  What for centuries now gives you the pleasure of gods:
Marshy banks here, where serried reeds have been
    growing for ages,
  Here all around the dark hills, shaded by bushes and
    trees.
First they showed but very few huts; then one day you
    saw them
  Spring to life as the race of fortunate plunderers
    swarmed. 40
All was booty to them and all was dragged to this city,
  So that the rest of the globe hardly deserved that you
    looked.
Here first you saw a new world, and then saw a world
    here in ruins,
  Then from ruins once more almost a still greater world!
So that I may see this one beneath your light for much
    longer 45
  Grant me that Clotho be slow spinning the thread of
    my life;
But let that one thing come quick, that hour so prettily
    signalled! –
  Happy! Did it just strike? No; but already it's Three.
Thus, beloved Muses, once more you came and beguiled
    me,
  Charmed away this long wait whilst I'm apart from my
    love. 50
Now farewell! I hurry and know I do not offend you;
  For, though proud, you agree Amor has always first
    place.

Venetian Epigrams (1790)

I

Sarcophagus, ampulla, the pagan chose life to adorn
them:
Fauns are dancing about, making a gaudy bright ring
With the Bacchantes' chorus; that goat-footed one of a
fat-face
Blasts the throaty hoarse notes wild from his shattering
horn.
Cymbals, tambours are clanging; we see and we hear in
the marble. 5
Birds in a flutter! that fruit, splendid it tastes to the
beak!
You're not scared off by noise, still less can it frighten off
Amor,
Needing a revelling crowd if he's to play with his torch.
Thus by abundance is death overcome; and the ashes
inside them
Seem, in silence enclosed, still to rejoice in this life. 10
Thus let this later scroll enwrap the tomb of the poet,
These inscriptions of his, patterned so richly with life.

VIII

See this gondola like to a cradle rocking so gently,
And the casket on top seems like a coffin with room.
Just so! In between cradle and coffin we haver and hover
Here on life's grand canal thoughtlessly floating along.

XXXVI

I was sated and weary with looking at paintings forever,
Marvellous treasures of art such as in Venice abound.
From this pleasure as well some rest and recovery's
needed;
And my languishing eye looked for some living delight.
Sorceress! then I could see in you those cherubims' model, 5
Just like Bellini portrays, painted with wings that
enchant,

Just as Paul Veronese will send them with cups to the bridegroom
And to the guests who enjoy, deluded, the water as wine.

XXXVII

How, from an exquisite artist's hand, the dear little figure,
Soft and without any bones, mollusc-like simply swims!
Everything's limb, and everything's joint, and everything's pleasing,
Everything measured to scale, everything moves as it wills.
Many humans I've known, and animals, birds, many fishes, 5
Many peculiar reptiles, great nature's marvellous works;
And yet I'm astonished by you, Bettina, dearest of marvels,
You who are all things at once, and an angel as well.

XLI

So will Breughel with figures tangled by primitive whimsy,
Hellish and sombre in mood, muddle our wavering sight;
So will Dürer convulse us with apocalyptic pictures,
Humans and fancies combined, sapping the health of our brains;
So a poet excites us, of sphinxes and sirens and centaurs 5
Singing, will maze wonders and will astonish the ear;
So a dream will disturb the careful one; thinking of holding,
Stepping straight on ahead, all tilts unstable and sways:
So Bettina confuses, her beauteous limbs all a-changing;
But we're instantly glad when she steps back on her feet. 10

XLII

How I'd exceed all the limits, outlined in chalk quite distinctly.
When she's performing the child courteously pushes me back.

XLIV

I like to watch all the things that you do; but best I like watching
When your father, adroit, tosses you head over heels,
You turning somersaults fly and from the *salto mortale*
Once more stand up and run, just as if nothing had been.

XLVII

'What's this madness that's hit your indolence? Why don't you stop it?
Shall this girl be a book? Play a more sensible tune!'
Patience, I'll sing about kings very soon, the world and its great ones,
Once I can grasp their craft better than now I can do.
But for now Bettina's my song; for jugglers and poets 5
Are so closely akin, seek out and find their own kind.

LXVIII

Think of lizards you've seen to picture the exquisite girls there
Rightly, all over the square moving now here and now there.
Quick and mercurial they are and gliding, standing and chatting,
And there's rustle of skirt trailed as they hurry away.
Look, she's there now! and there! If once you should lose her it's useless 5
To keep seeking; she won't come back so quickly again.
If however you fear no dark nooks, nor alleys and stairways,
Go then, follow her lure, where the tavern invites!

LXX

Lizards, two of the finest, would always walk out with each other;
One of them almost too big, one of them almost too small.
If you see them together you can't choose one or the other;

Each one alone though appeared clearly the loveliest of all.

LXXVII

'Botanising passing your time? with optics? What's that for?
Are there not nicer rewards touching the sensitive hearts?'
Ah, the sensitive hearts now! a bungler is able to touch them;
Let this alone be my joy, Nature, to touch all of you!

XC

What a tease of a game! The disc on the thread is revolving,
Out of the hand escaped quickly it climbs back again!
See, it seems like my heart, to this fair beauty then that one
I may throw it; but then back in an instant it flies.

XCV

You're amazed and you point out the sea; it seems to be burning.
How the waves flood in flames here round the ship in the night!
I'm by no means surprised; the ocean bore Aphrodite,
And from her leaped to us surely a flame, her son?

CII

It's a delight, to be holding your love in your arms with her longing
Whilst the beat of her heart newly confesses her love.
Still more delight, to feel how the new live being is thumping
As it incessantly moves feeding within the sweet womb.
Even now like impetuous youth it's jumping; already 5
How impatient it knocks, longs to reach heavenly light.
Wait just a few more days longer! The Horae soon enough lead you

Strictly through all of life's paths, following Fate's stern command.
Whatsoever befall you in time, you dear little thriveling –
You were fashioned by Love; Love be your portion in life! 10

CIII

Thus I dallied with time, cut off from friends to divert me,
In the Neptunian town losing the hours and days.
All I experienced I spiced with my sweet recollections,
Spiced it with hope; they're the most exquisite spice in the world.

Withheld Venetian Epigrams (1790)

XLI

Exquisite rings I have purchased! Engraved and most excellent crystals,
Noble in style as in theme, clasped in the purest of gold.
Dearly those rings must be paid for that flash with the blazing of crystals
Such as often you've seen aglow on the gambling board.
But there's a ringlet I know of, that's quite a different story, 5
One Hans Carvel[6] when old one time so sadly possessed.
He unwisely the smallest of all his ten fingers inserted
There where worthily fits only the biggest, eleven.

LXX

In the narrowest alley – a slip one hardly could squeeze through –
Blocking my way sat a girl, when I walked Venice one day.

Fired by her, and the place, a stranger I then lost my
bearings;
Oh, how wide a canal opened for me to explore.
If you had girls like canals that you offer, O Venice, and
c—s 5
Like your alleys within, you'd be a city supreme.

Lover's Nearness (1796)

I think of you, whenever sun's bright shimmer
From ocean streams;
I think of you, whenever moon's soft glimmer
In wellsprings gleams.

I see you when, there on the distant ridgeway, 5
The dust-cloud blurs;
In deepest night, when on the narrow bridgeway
The wanderer stirs.

I hear you in the muffled sound of surging
When tide-wave fills; 10
In quiet grove I listen to the urging
When silence stills.

I am with you, though you be far and pining,
You are so near!
The sun goes down. The stars will soon be shining. 15
Would you were here!

The God and the Bayadere (1797)

Indian Legend

Lord of Earth, great Mahadeva,
Comes a sixth time down again,
Comes to feel with each believer
All our human joy and pain.
Here to dwell with us he pleases 5
To experience come what may.
As he punishes or eases
Mankind's lot he must essay.
And when in the town his inspection he's ended,
Has spied on the great, to the humble attended, 10
He leaves it at evening to go on his way.

When at very last he reaches
Houses on the city's bourn
There he sees the painted features
Of a lovely child forlorn. 15
'Greetings, Mistress!' – 'Praise I treasure!
I'll come out, do stay with me.' –
'Say who are you?' – 'Girl of pleasure;
This the house of love you see.'
She starts on her dance to the beat of the cymbal, 20
She graces the space as she circles so nimble,
She finely inclines as she ends on her knee.

To the threshold, charming sprightly,
To the house she leads him through.
'Stranger fair, soon lamplight-brightly 25
All this room will shine for you.
If you're tired I'll revive you,
Soothe and ease your feet that smart.
All your wants, I'll not deprive you,
Rest, or zest, or jest impart.' 30
The pains he pretends to she's quickly relieving.
The god looks on smiling, with pleasure perceiving
In depth of corruption so human a heart.

Slave-girl duties he arranges
But she only grows more gay, 35
And what was her art now changes
By and by to nature's way.
So the flower bloomed and fruited,
Naturally her gifts appear:
Where obedience is rooted 40
Love as well is very near.
But testing her closer more sharp ways he uses,
Heights and the depths he knows well and he chooses
Pleasure and terror and torments to fear.

On daubed cheeks his kisses showered, 45
And she feels a love that sears,
And the girl stands overpowered
And the first time she sheds tears;
At his feet she sinks down humbly,
Not for lust, and not for gain; 50
Ah, the limbs once lithe and comely
Fail her as her spirits wane.
Then hours of the night for the deep consummation
Spread softly a veil round the sweet celebration
In loveliness spun from their ample dark skein. 55

Late to sleep, with heart's tease vying,
Waking early from short rest
Close beside her she finds lying
Dead her dearest much-loved guest.
And her screams cannot restore him 60
As she clasps her heart's desire;
Cold and rigid he, they bore him
Swiftly to the funeral fire.
She hears the intoning, the priests and the dirges,
In frenzy she thrusts through the crowd as it surges. 65
'Who are you? By what right are you at the pyre?'

By the bier she falls down shrieking,
Cries that pierce through all the sky:
'This my husband I am seeking!
Give him back, I tomb defy. 70

Shall these limbs be ash and smother,
This divine and splendid sight?
Mine! he was! for no one other!
Oh, for only One sweet night!'
The priests go on chanting: 'The aged are taken, 75
Long wearied and finally cold and forsaken,
The young ones are taken surprised in full flight.

Hear your priests and hear our ruling:
This was not your husband true.
Bayadere are you by schooling 80
So no duty lies on you.
Only shade with corpse united
Rights in death's hushed realm can claim,
Only wife to husband plighted:
That is duty, that is fame. 85
Sound, trumpet, the sacred and sad lamentation!
O gods, take this jewel of time's brief duration,
O take to your keeping the youth in this flame!'

Ruthless chorus, that augmented
Anguish in her every breath; 90
Arms outstretched she leaps tormented
To the burning blaze of death.
But the god-youth freely soaring
From the flames ascends the sky;
With him, in his arms restoring, 95
His beloved floats on high.
For penitent sinners divinity jubilates;
Immortals lift children of darkness that desolates
In burning embraces to heaven on high.

The Metamorphosis of Plants (June 1798)

This confuses you, dearest, these modes of thousands of minglings
In the riotous flowers spread through the garden all round;
Many names you hear with respect, and each one's barbaric
Sound will always displace each that you heard just before.
All forms are like in their structure, and none equates with the other; 5
And this common accord points to mysterious law,
To a sacred enigma. O could I, my dearest companion,
Give you one happy word apt to resolve all at once!
Watch as it comes into being, see how the plant through progression,
Guided step-wise along, forms into flowers and fruit. 10
It develops at once from the seed as soon as the quiet
Life-giving womb of the earth bids it go free into life
And to stimulant light, the sacred, for ever in motion,
It trusts the delicate work of making the burgeoning leaves.
Simple the force asleep in the seed; an incipient model 15
Lay, enclosed in itself, curled up there under the sheath,
Leaf and rootlet and bud, only half-formed with no colour;
Thus the kernel sustains tranquil life in the dry,
Straining upward it swells, on gentle moisture relying,
Quickly lifting itself from the encompassing night. 20
But the form remains in its first appearance still simple;
And so the plants too show features denoting the child.
Straightaway a following thrust, rising likewise, renews it,
Piling up node upon node, always that first innate form.
Though not always the same one; for always leaves that come after 25

Differ, as you can see, reproduce manifold,
More extended, more dented, more split into tips and with members
Which before had been joined when in the organ below.
And thus it reaches at first the most specific perfection
Which in many a kind moves and astonishes you. 30
Much serrated and ribbed, on gorged and swelling surface,
Now the abundance of thrust seems to be endless and free.
Here though with hands overpowering nature reins back the force
That shapes, and steers it smooth to make it more perfect still.
Moderate now it conducts the sap, and narrows the vessels, 35
The form showing at once much more delicate effects.
Gradually the thrust recedes from the onpushing edges
And the rib of the stalk takes on more fullness and girth.
Leafless now though and quick the stem more delicate rises
And a marvel of form holds the observer enthralled. 40
Forming a circle they take their place, all counted yet past all
Counting, leaves much more small stand next to similar leaves.
Round the axis compressed the sheltering calyx develops
And, for ultimate form, coloured corollas emits.
Nature thus comes to flaunt in full and highest appearance, 45
Showing, ordered in steps, members on members arranged.
Always newly it stuns you as soon as the flower starts moving
Over the varying leaves' scaffold built light round the stem.
But this great glory speaks to proclaim still newer creating;
Yes, the bright coloured leaf senses divinity's hand 50

And it quickly draws itself in; most delicate forms now,
  Twinned they push themselves through, destined and made to unite.
Harmoniously they stand, the gracious couples, together,
  Numerously arranged all round the altar divine.
Hymen hovers above, and splendours of fragrance, compelling, 55
  Pour sweet odours around quickening all things with life.
Separated, numberless seeds at once begin swelling
  Wrapped in the swelling fruits' tenderly mothering womb.
And here nature completes the ring of perpetual forces;
  But a new one at once seizes the previous one 60
So that the chain carries on and through all ages continues
  Whereby the whole can become, like the particular, live.
Look again, O my dearest, and watch the colourful turmoil,
  Which confuses no more as in the mind's eye it moves.
Now every plant will proclaim to you the laws everlasting, 65
  Every flower will speak louder and louder to you.
If you decipher it here, the sacred script of the goddess,
  Everywhere it appears, even when altered in style.
The hesitant larva may crawl, the butterfly busily hurry,
  Malleable man himself transform his own given form. 70
O be mindful as well, how from the seed of acquaintance
  Bud by bud in us a sweetest accustoming sprang,
Friendship with such power emerged from deep down within us,
  And how Amor at last flowers and fruit has produced.
Think too how nature forms now this, now that way our feelings, 75
  Here too you can observe forms as they quietly unfold!
Also rejoice in this day! For love ever sacred aspires
  To produce in like minds fruit of the highest degree,
In a likeness of view so in harmonious vision
  Joined the pair may unite, rise to that high other world. 80

World Soul[7] (1798–1802)

Depart this feast of sacred dedication
And search all worlds about!
Rush through the universe in pure elation,
Enthuse and fill it out!

In blissful soaring through unfathomed distance 5
The dream of gods you dream,
With stars and seeding light in new existence
You join in space and gleam.

Then, mighty comets, thrusting through the notion
Of far and further space 10
You intersect the labyrinthine motion
That suns and planets pace.

You snatch and grasp for worlds not yet created
With youth's productive urge,
So that they live for ever animated 15
With every measured surge.

Through eddied airs you circle firmly guiding
The plant that changing grows,
You rule the stone in deepest caverns hiding
And stable forms impose. 20

Their nature to surpass with godlike power
Now all things boldly strive;
And water, barren, wants to green and flower,
Each speck of dust's alive.

Thus banish by your efforts, caring, steady, 25
The dank and murk of night;
Now Paradise in splendours glows already
Exuberantly bright.

How soon to see the grace of light life presses,
How hosts of forms are raised, 30
And now you stand on smiling fields it blesses
As earth's first pair amazed.

Soon impulse ebbs in joy's reciprocation,
In bliss of eye and soul.
And so receive with thanks life's consummation 35
In Wholeness from the Whole.

[Nature and Art] (1800)

Though art and nature seem sore disunited
Yet each, before you think, to each is turning;
I too no longer sense discordant spurning,
By equal pulls seem equally excited.

An honest effort's bound to be requited! 5
If measured hours we dedicate to learning
And bind ourselves to art with zeal discerning
The heart may glow with nature new ignited.

So too all forming culture needs some tether:
Unbridled spirits end in vain disaster 10
Pursuing pure perfection's elevation.

Who wants great things must get himself together;
Constraint is where you show you are a master,
And only law is freedom's sure foundation.

When spring's gold sunshine hours enspelled me (1800)

When spring's gold sunshine hours enspelled me
This vision held me
In raptured mood.
In the senses' dark and fruitful teeming
I was able to start this dreaming, 5
But not conclude.

from To the New Year (1801)

Old Year is passing,
New Year is waiting,
We're celebrating
Good fortune today;
What's past finds its meaning 5
When trust is our tutor
In seeing the future
And the past's true assay.

Others see only
The Old Year shadowed, 10
Wrinkled and harrowed,
Sad fearful mood;
We though see shining
Friendship and trusting;
See, the New thrusting 15
Finds us renewed!

Lasting Change (1803)

Oh, if only springtime's blessing
Could be held for just one hour!
But the mild west wind is pressing
And already blossoms shower.
All this green, should I enjoy it, 5
Grateful for its recent shade?
Autumn's storms will soon destroy it
Once it's rocked the leaves that fade.

From the fruits your share ensuring
Grasp them quickly as you need! 10
These ones here begin maturing
And already others seed;
See your lovely valley quiver,
Altering instantly in rain;
Oh, and in the self-same river 15
You will never swim again.

And now you! Those things you reckoned
Firm as mountains in the skies,
Walls and palaces each second
You will see with other eyes. 20
Gone the lip which found in kisses
Healing in those former times,
And bold foot from precipices
Where the mountain goat still climbs.

And that hand, with warm devotion 25
Always opening good to do,
Membered living form in motion,
Now all that's some other too.
And whatever all displaces –
That to which your name's now lent – 30
Came here like a wave that races
Onwards to the element.

Let the start and end so fusing
Join in One and unify!
Swifter than the things you're losing 35
You must let yourself go by!
Thank the Muses for bestowing
Favour of a lasting kind:
Import from your heart outflowing
And the form within your mind. 40

Whatever you think truth or fable (1805)

Whatever you think truth or fable
That in a thousand books you find
It all remains a Tower of Babel
Unless it is by love combined.

Sonnet Cycle (1807–8)

I
Unexpected Overwhelming

From clouded rocky vaults a river gushes,
To join the distant ocean downwards racing:
Its course unchecked through mirrored valleys tracing,
Into the valley on and on it pushes.

But Oreas, daimonic, sudden rushes – 5
With cliff and forest too in whirlwinds chasing –
To seek contentment in that flow's embracing
And halts it, forms a vessel ringed with bushes.

The wave spurts foam and then retreats, astounded,
And drinks itself in swirl of backwards streaming; 10
The striving to the Father is abated.

It sways and rests, and as a lake is bounded;
The constellations, mirrored, watch the gleaming
As wave laps rock, as new life is created.

II
Friendly Meeting

Enveloped in my cloak, the serpentining
Track I traced that fell through mist and boulder
To wintering fields below and ever colder;
Escape was all my restless mind's inclining.

Then suddenly there was a new day shining: 5
A girl appeared; transported I behold her
Exemplary as poet's liege from older
And fabled times. It quieted my pining.

I let her pass and turned away, misguided,
More tightly wrapped myself in folds constraining 10
Like one whose scorn all other warmth replaces;

Yet followed her. She stopped. Then fate decided.
No longer in my cloak myself containing
I cast it off, she lay in my embraces.

III
Enough

Should I with her completely be contented?
I'd finish up with only irritation.
That's why today I'll try some abnegation
And from her customed beauty be absented.

My heart, I did not ask if you assented; 5
For such grave fault what reconciliation?
So be it! Come! Our loving lamentation
In sounds serenely sad shall be presented.

You see, it works! We're half-anticipated,
The poet's muse already rhapsodises 10
On selfless love with melodies endearing.

You've hardly thought, and see, the song's created;
What now? – I think while this fresh fire surprises
We'll hurry off and sing it in her hearing.

IV
The Girl Speaks

You look so stern, my love! as here reflected
In this, your marble bust, that prompts comparing:
Like it you give no sign of life or caring,
Yet stone seems softer and the more affected.

The foe will take a shield to be protected, 5
The friend should have a frankly open bearing.
I seek you, you draw back as from a snaring;
Stand firm now, like this work that art perfected.

And now to which one should I look for favour?
Must I by both alike be treated coldly 10
When this is dead but you have life that warms you?

Enough, with idle talk I'll no more haver;
And so I'll kiss this marble statue boldly
Until you drag me off as envy storms you.

V
Growth

With you, a little skipping child, I'd wander
With springtime dawn the fields and meadows sharing.
'For such a daughter I'd be quite unsparing,
To build her houses all my wealth I'd squander!'

When later you on life began to ponder 5
Your pleasure was for household tasks preparing.
'With such a sister! she would be so caring:
In our confiding each would be the fonder!'

Now for that lovely growth there's no confining;
My heart endures love's raging conflagration. 10
Should I embrace her, from such pains to ease me?

Alas! as for a princess now I'm pining:
Abruptly, now you're high above my station;
I bow before your glance that hardly sees me.

VI
Provisions

I had to leave those looks from her I needed,
That radiance and my life's illumination.
What we call fate brooks no accommodation;
So I withdrew and to fate's shock conceded.

All other happiness was superseded; 5
At once I exercised renunciation,
Of this and that need practised deprivation:
Those looks from her alone seemed all I needed.

The warmth of wine, food's relish, gifts unnumbered,
Companions, comforts, sleep, all now redundant! 10
I cast them off, the minimum retaining.

At ease I walk the world now, unencumbered:
To meet my need the world has stuff abundant;
I carry what's essential – love's sustaining.

VII
Parting

From many thousand kisses still unsated
There came with one last kiss the separation.
And after parting's bitter immolation
I pulled off from the shore while pain abated

As houses, mountains, streams I contemplated, 5
To see them was a treasured compensation;
Then eye's delight, the distant indication
Of blue horizons darkly animated.

Until my heart was scorched again by yearning,
To see at last the open sea before me; 10
I searched for all I'd lost with grim obsession.

Then suddenly it seemed the heavens were burning;
I'd nothing lost, and wholly to restore me
All previous joys returned as my possession.

VIII
His Love Writes

One look from yours to mine your love imparted,
Your mouth on mine one single kiss bestowing;
For such as me, and after such a knowing,
Can any other happiness be charted?

So far from you, from all my near ones parted, 5
I watch my thoughts that circle to and froing
Forever to that single hour flowing,
The only one: and now my tears have started.

But unexpectedly my tears are ending;
His love, I think, breaks through my isolation 10
So should you not reach him with words unspoken?

Hear now this whispered breath of love I'm sending!
My only fortune and my consolation
Is your fond will; oh send to me some token!

IX
His Love Writes Again

Another note, and what am I intending?
That point, my love, you mustn't want decided:
For though there's nothing new to be confided
This note you'll hold in hands all comprehending.

As I can't come this paper that I'm sending 5
Conveys to you my whole heart undivided,
By joys and hopes, delights and torments guided:
All that has no beginning, has no ending.

I can't tell of my day, how I adore you,
My sensing, wishing, dreams, and what I've wanted, 10
All day my faithful heart to you directed:

Once, just to look at you, I stood before you
And said no word. And what would words have counted?
I knew then all my being was perfected.

X
She Cannot End

If I were now this empty white sheet sending
Without first covering it with any writing
Perhaps you'd find to write on it inviting
And send it me whose joys you make unending.

As woman will, impulsively dependent, 5
I'd tear the envelope, be so excited
To know what's hidden and I'd be delighted
To read, as you once said them, words transcendent:

'Dear child! My sweetest heart! My only being!'
So you would spoil me with sweet words adoring 10
And still my yearning when we were together.

Your murmuring as well I'd think I'm seeing
As when you filled my soul, your love outpouring,
In me my beauty imaging for ever.

XI
Nemesis

When all the nation's by fierce plague infected
It's best to stay in prudent isolation.
And by omission and by hesitation
From influences I have stayed protected.

By Amor often favoured and selected 5
I found with him no lasting occupation.
And so it was with all that 'Lachrymation'[8]
When three- and fourfold rhyming was expected.

But he who scorns finds punishment comes after,
As by the Furies' snaking torch tormented 10
From hill to vale, from land to sea he's driven.

Yet though I hear the Spirits' scornful laughter
It does not sober me since I'm demented,
By sonnet mania and love's madness riven.

XII
Christmas Present

My sweetest love! Here for your Christmas platter
Accept the varied sweets this carton's bearing.
They're fruits we bake for children, so declaring
That Christmas is a sweet and holy matter!

Poetic sweetmeats in rhetoric chatter, 5
This festival for you I've been preparing;
Yet for such vanities as these, who's caring?
Away with this attempt to blind and flatter!

But from within and inwardly to meet you,
Erasing distance, come sweet consolations 10
That only in the air can be detected.

If you then feel dear memories that greet you
As from the shine of well-known constellations
I trust these smaller gifts won't be rejected.

XIII
Warning

On that Last Day when loud the trumpet's sounded
And this our earthly life must be surrendered,
Account must then for every word be rendered
Which uselessly my vanity compounded.

Then by my many words shall I be foundered 5
Which striving for your grace in me engendered
And I so lovingly to you have tendered?
What then, if all my words should prove ungrounded?

Consider then what conscience now refuses,
Consider, dearest, how you've hesitated, 10
That by such pain our world be not offended.

If I must calculate and make excuses
For all the words on you I've dissipated
That Last Day to a year must be extended.

XIV
Doubters:

You love, and so write sonnets! All's pretended!
You think that coupling rhymes in such composing
Can sate the heart that craves the heart's disclosing;
Believe us, dears, you'll find your will's suspended.

Not even words whose flow is never ended 5
Can tell heart's plenitude: it likes reposing;
Then storm-like all the strings and stops disposing;
Then being again to still of night surrendered.

Why torture then yourselves and us who read you
To push the stone uphill in steps so tiring 10
Whilst back it rolls and makes the struggle harder?

Lovers:

Our way is right, so don't let that mislead you!
To melt the hardest stuff needs only firing
By all-consuming love's commanding ardour.

XV
Girl:

I doubt the worth of lines all interlacing!
Agreed, I find your wordplay's most appealing;
But surely what our hearts are truly feeling
Should not, my sweet, be wrought in bevelled casing.

The poet delves, when tedious themes replacing, 5
To churn his substance inside out revealing;
But for his wounds he knows a cooling healing,
The spell of words, his deepest scars effacing.

Poet:

But look, my dear, the sapper: how's his calling?
His training's to discharge a measured thunder, 10
The skill with which he drives his shafts amazes.

However, elemental power's appalling,
And suddenly with all his craft asunder
He's blown into the air and gone to blazes.

XVI
Epoch

In Petrarch's heart Good Friday's conflagration
Inscribed a testament forever burning.
So Advent was my own time's overturning
In Eighteen Seven, my year of exaltation.

It was no start, just love's continuation, 5
For her my heart much earlier was yearning
Till later on it turned to prudent spurning,
And now her heart's my lasting inclination.

Yet Petrarch's love, though infinite its soaring,
Was really sad and sadly unrewarded, 10
Eternally Good Friday's heart in mourning.

But let my lady come, with bliss outpouring,
Let gladly palms triumphant be accorded,
So on and on eternal Mayday dawning.

XVII
Charade[9]

Just two short words, and easy their expression,
How often with pure joy they've been recited
Although the seals are never clearly sighted
That stamp on them their meaning's true impression.

The days of youth and age we like to freshen 5
By boldly getting each by each ignited;
And if in one name they can be united
They sound like our well-being's glad confession.

But now I look for them in play that pleases
And hope their pleasure's into mine projected; 10
And silently I hope I'll soon be seeing:

In them my own love's name in mask that teases,
ONE image where they both can be detected
And I can both embrace in that ONE being.

Unless the eye had sunlike parts (1810)

Unless the eye had sunlike parts
It could not see the sun and sight us;
Unless the god's own power were in our hearts
How could what is divine delight us?

The Diary (1810)

I had another woman in my arms, but when
I was about to enjoy her, Venus called to mind my lady
and left me in the lurch.[10]

We hear it said and in the end believe it:
The human heart's unfathomable for ever,
And Christians, heathens, though they can't conceive it
Are all in sinful nature one together.
It's best that we shake hands on that and leave it, 5
That we don't chafe ourselves on doctrine's tether;
For though some spirit brings us in temptation
Some power still guards our virtue and salvation.

For long from my own darling separated,
As often happens, on some business dealing, 10
I earned and learned, was wined and dined and feted,
But I kept only her in thought and feeling:
It's night when sky by stars is penetrated
And far love grows in memory's unsealing,
And that's when I would pen to her my greeting, 15
In loving words each day's events repeating.

So now I hurried back. My carriage failed me,
It broke, and all my thoughts of home receded
By one more night, and such a rage assailed me
When work and patience were the things I needed. 20
The smith and wheelwright worked, no words availed me,
They held their tongue, my fury went unheeded.
Each craft has got its foibles, fads and fumble.
What then my role? None left but wait and grumble.

So there I was. The Star Inn's sign invited, 25
It really seemed not bad accommodation.
A girl, whose form superlative I sighted,
Brought light. I felt a cosy warm sensation.
By pleasant hall and stairs I was delighted,
By little rooms beyond all expectation. 30
When sinful man soars free how that refreshes –
Then beauty spins and takes him in her meshes.

And then I took the diary I'd been keeping
To please my darling with the usual letter
I loved to write her when the world was sleeping, 35
For then, alone with her, my words flowed better;
But somehow now my words were only creeping
As though my pen was troubled by some fetter:
The girl arrived and laid my supper-table
With courteous greetings, dignified and able. 40

She comes and goes. I speak, she speaks politely;
She seems more fair with every word she answers.
And as she carves my chicken, deft and lightly,
The grace of moving hand and arm entrances –

The stuff that makes the nonsense in us sprightly – 45
Enough, I'm lost, I'm mad, all reels and dances,
I leap up, chair knocked down, some force impels me
To grasp her: 'Don't, please don't' her whisper tells me;

'My aunt's downstairs, a dragon old and vicious,
She counts each minute, soon she'll be complaining; 50
When I'm up here she thinks and grows suspicious,
Each time I'm late I get another caning.
Don't lock your door, keep watch, and be judicious
Till midnight, then we'll both need no restraining.'
She struggles free and hurries out, all harassed; 55
Then later back, she serves me, unembarrassed

But with such looks! So that each look confesses,
Such heavenly promises each one proposes,
There's not one quiet sigh that she represses,
Each stirs her bosom, rounds it and discloses. 60
I see on ear, on neck, in nape's recesses
Love's blossom in the fleeting tint of roses.
She sees no more to do, looks round, half-hearted,
One hesitation more and she's departed.

In house and streets now midnight's peace is flowing; 65
Although for me a wide bed is provided
Love prompts, as ever good advice bestowing,
So mine's the smallest portion I've decided.
I hesitate then leave the candles glowing,
I hear her, though so quietly she's glided, 70
My passioned eyes explore her form exalted,
She lies down close, I clasp her form unfaulted.

She frees herself: 'First hear my explanation,
Then take me knowing all, no false pretences.
It doesn't look so, but my past relation 75
To men was timid, I was all defences.
Round here I have a prudish reputation;
My heart's now changed, you've brought me to my senses:
You've conquered me, so don't let it annoy you
That I saw, I loved, and swore that I'd enjoy you. 80

You take me pure, and were it in my power
I'd give you more if I knew more what pleases.'
Her sweet breasts press my breast, as though this hour
With me for her was all of all that eases.
On mouth and eyes and brow my kisses shower, 85
Then fate devised the oddest of his teases:
For he who's used to play the heated Master
As schoolboys do draws back and cools off faster.

It seems that tender words and soft caresses
Fulfil her heart from love so long absented. 90
Her body's sweet abundance chasteness blesses
And all to me she lovingly consented!
Such joyfulness and rapture she expresses
And then she rests as if she were contented.
I rested too, my fond gaze on her figure, 95
My hope and trust still with the Master's vigour.

I pondered my misfortune ill-encumbered,
In all my seething soul dark spirits snickered
And mocked, with curses, grins and jeers unnumbered,
And as I dithered, on and on they bickered 100
While she, more fair than when awake, just slumbered
As, lower now, the wavering candles flickered.
To youth that sweats and toils in daily labour
Sweet sleep comes easy as a welcome neighbour.

In comfort thus she lay like heaven's daughter 105
As if all hers the bed where she was lying,
And feeble, squashed against the wall's rough mortar,
The one to whom she nothing was denying.
Thus snakebite kills, just when he's reached the water,
The traveller of thirst already dying. 110
She dreams a dream in her own gracious making;
He holds his breath lest she have stir or waking.

He tells himself, this first time he's found failing:
You too now know why, fearing they'll be haltered,
Those bridegrooms cross themselves, in spirit quailing 115
Lest they by baleful knots be snared and faulted.

Far best the battlefield and bullets hailing
Than here disgraced! Since long ago you've altered
Since first, in blazing pomp of light surrounded,
You saw your lady-liege and were astounded. 120

Your heart and senses surged and pricked and heated,
The whole man all ecstatically excited.
You rushed her off to dance, you'd scarcely greeted,
To hold at once as all of you delighted,
As though you with yourself for her competed; 125
Your powers multiplied that she ignited:
Your mind, wit, vital spirits, quickened faster,
And of them all the quickest was that Master.

Desire and inclination grew, compelling,
And early in the spring our troth was plighted, 130
Herself the fairest flowers of May excelling;
An eager pair, young appetites unblighted!
And when at last we wed – the truth needs telling –
Before the altar where we were united,
Before your anguished cross where you were martyred, 135
Dear Lord forgive me, That One stirred and started.[11]

You sumptuous bed, you pillows broad, that bore us
That bridal night when we became each other's,
You tapestries that, when urgent love would soar us
In passioned joys, would hide us in silk covers! 140
You cage-birds, never soon enough your chorus
That woke us to renew the zest of lovers!
You knew us well, at ease in your safe tending,
Her taking her fond part, me never ending.

And often later, when we'd be securing 145
In secret holy wedlock's rights so gracious,
In sedge's screen, in waves of corn maturing,
And less fit places where I'd grow audacious,
We got such instant service reassuring
From that fine servant, tirelessly vivacious! 150
Damned wretch, in endless stupor you're prostrated!
Your lord's best happiness you've now frustrated.

Now Master That One's moodiness bemuses,
He'll not take orders nor brook any spurning,
But suddenly he's there, and quietly chooses 155
To raise himself, to splendrous form returning;
Thus freed, the traveller that parched prospect loses
Of all night by the well in thirsty burning.
He leans to kiss the sleeping girl who draws him
But stops, he feels pulled back, some power awes him. 160

Who else has spurred his strength re-animated
Than she, whose cherished value never ceases,
He wed in youth's untethered zest unsated?
Her fire anew its freshening releases,
And as, when feeble first, his torments baited 165
So now, when strong, his awed unease increases;
Then fearful, cautious, quiet, quiet, he's leaving
That zone enspelled in grace and magic's weaving.

He sits, writes: 'Near home I met with more delaying,
Chance took me further from my destination, 170
But here, in this strange place where I've been staying,
I've pledged to you my heart's re-dedication.
I'll end this letter with this secret saying:
Only by sickness is health validated.
Of many a good my words to you have spoken, 175
The best must stay in silence never broken.'

The cockerel crows. At once she swiftly pushes
The sheets off, throws her dress on, still half-dreaming.
She startles, looks, lowers her eyes and blushes,
Her being there feels strange and not quite seeming; 180
And as this final time away she rushes
His eyes still hold her lovely body's gleaming:
The post-horn sounds; he rides along in pleasure
With heart restored to greet his love and treasure.

And since at last all poetry's a fable 185
That needs some moral that is edifying,

My verse shall try as much as it is able
To gladly tell the point that's underlying:
In earth's mad business stumbling and unstable
We yet find much is done, there's no denying, 190
By two strong powers within us and above:
By *Duty* much, endlessly more by *Love*!

[A Dying Fly] (1810)

How avidly it goes on sucking steady
The treacherous drink, seduced by that first taste;
It feels so well, though paralysed already
In jointed legs minute and finely traced;
No longer agile, tiny wings to spangle, 5
No longer able little head to angle –
Thus lost in its enjoyment life must waste.
The little foot will soon be feebly listing;
And so it gulps for more, its suck persisting
As death round all its thousand eyes is misting. 10

Presence (1812)

All things tell when you come!
So when the sun shines in its splendour
You will, I hope, follow soon.

If in the garden you walk
Then you are the rose of all roses, 5
Lily of lilies as well,

And as you move when you dance
The constellate stars will dance with you
And all around you at once.

Night! and so let it be night! 10
Now you'll outshine the moon's lovely
Luminous welcoming sheen.

Welcoming lovely you are
And flowers, moon, and the starlight
Venerate, sun, only you. 15

Sun! be that also for me,
Creator of days of great splendour;
Life and eternity's there.

What God would nudge his world but not be in it (1812)

What God would nudge his world but not be in it
And only round his finger twirl and spin it!
He moves the world by inwardly impelling,
And He is nature's, nature His, indwelling
So that what in Him lives and works and is 5
Can't lack the power and spirit that are His.

Within us too a universe we find;
Hence, laudably, that custom of mankind
That each will give his own ideal the name
Of God, as his own God proclaim, 10
Will give Him earth and heaven above,
Will fear Him and may even love.

from **Friendly Xenia VI** (1815–27)

My stature is my Father's part,
Life's earnest from the cradle;
From Mother I've my sunny heart
And fancy for a fable.
Great-grandpa had an eye for girls, 5
At times in me it itches;
Great-grandma fancied gold and pearls,
An urge all through for riches.
These parts make up a man like me
And can't be separated, 10
So where's originality
In what a chap's created?

Spring All Year Through (1816)

The loosening flower-bed
Lets itself go,
Small bells are swaying
All white as snow;
Crocus releases 5
From emerald bud
A glowing power
And burgeons blood.
Primroses pertly
Parade and prance, 10
Violet teases
And looks askance;
Whatever's stirring
With might and main,
Spring's up and doing 15
And live again.

But where the garden's
Richness excels
Is where my darling's
Dear presence dwells. 20
Those looks that warm me
And ever fire,
To song excite me,
To word inspire:
A heart that flowers, 25
That's open and clear,
In earnest kindly,
In jest sincere.
Though rose and lily
Take summer's part 30
My love's the winner
That holds my heart.

Memorial (1816)

There on shores where no life's thriving,
Where dune piles on dune in heaps,
Where the storm in darkness seeps,
Let your aim be onward striving.
Under cyphers long since smothered 5
Forebears thousandfold lie still,
Oh! now new fresh mounds have covered
Friend on friends in death's deep chill.

Thus accept our life so fated
Then may night and sky grow bright 10
And stars' thronged eternal light
Mean to you hours animated,
Whilst with others here untroubled
You stay loyal, active, kind
Hurrying with love redoubled 15
Loved eternal ones to find.

Primal Words, Orphic (1817)

ΔΑΙΜΩΝ, Daimon

When you were granted here your brief admission,
As sun and planets met that day they charted
For evermore your growing to fruition
According to the law by which you started.
Thus must you be, from self there's no remission, 5
Thus long have sibyls, prophets this imparted;
Nor any time nor any power can shatter
Imprinted form informing living matter.

ΤΥΧΗ, Chance

But easing change gets round that stern constriction
As with and round us change is all-imbuing; 10
No more alone, you grow through social friction
And do such deeds as any man is doing.
This life's an ebb and flow, a contradiction,
A toy that's toyed with, play for our pursuing.
The years have quietly formed the circle's essence, 15
The lamp awaits the flame of incandescence.

ΕΡΩΣ, Love

And come it must! – He plunges earthwards winging
Who from the timeless void to heaven once sped,
On airy pinions hovering and swinging
All springtime's day around the heart and head, 20
Away and back again forever springing,
Then woe is weal, there's sweet delights in dread.
So many soaring hearts are dissipated,
The noblest to the One is dedicated.

ΑΝΑΓΚΗ, Necessity

Then back once more, to what the stars had fated: 25
Conditioning and law; and wish from willing
Can only come since we are obligated,
Our will then all our fitful fancies killing;

Its dearest from the heart is extirpated,
Hard 'Must' prevails, both will and fancy stilling. 30
Thus, though we seem free, yet constrictions bind us
More closely still than those that first confined us.

ΕΛΠΙΣ, Hope

But such a confine, such a wall immuring
In odious chafe, is breached and left ungated
Though like the timeless crags it seem enduring! 35
A Being rises light and liberated:
Through showering rain and cloud and mist obscuring
She lifts us up, we soar on wings elated:
You know her well, ranging all zones to find us;
One wingbeat – and the aeons lie behind us! 40

At Midnight (1818)

At midnight I would walk, but very wary,
Across that churchyard, such a small small boy,
To father's house, the parson's; stars all starry,
Their really lovely sparkling was such joy;
At midnight. 5

And when I later then in life's extension
Was forced to her, was forced by love's intent,
The stars and Northern Lights in high contention,
I'd savour coming blisses as I went;
At midnight. 10

Until at last the moon in fullness shining
My darkness pierced, so clearly and defined;
Then thought, all willing, sensing, leaped combining
Both past and future instantly in mind;
At midnight. 15

Epirrhema[12] (1819)

If you'd look at nature truly
One as all examine duly!
No thing's inside, outside neither:
In is out and both are either.
Grasp it quick, let nought confound you, 5
Sacred secret all around you.

*

True appearance, earnest game,
Joys in them discover:
Nothing living is one and the same,
It's always many another! 10

Antepirrhema (1819)

Now humbly observe as she without cease
Eternally weaves her masterpiece,
One tread, a thousand threads respond,
The shuttles shoot swiftly to and froing,
The joining threads run onwards flowing, 5
One throw a thousand links will bond!
She hasn't just now scraped that together,
In eternity she planned it for ever;
So that the eternal craftsman will know
That all is well when he makes his throw. 10

Eve of St Nepomuk[13] (1820)

Karlsbad, 15 May 1820

Lanterns float downstream a-twinkle,
Children on the bridge are singing,
Big bell, small bell, peal and tinkle,
All delight and reverence ringing.

Lanterns fade, the stars are fading; 5
So was loosed the soul sure-guided
Of our saint, whom no persuading
Forced to speak of faults confided.

Lanterns, float on! children, play then!
Children's choir, o sing it singing! 10
And no less proclaim and say then
Why this star to stars is winging.

Wilhelm Tischbein's Idylls (1821)

I

Noble splendid buildings tumble,
Walls collapse round vaults still standing,
After centuries commanding
Entrances and pillars crumble.
Life then starts itself restoring, 5
Earth and new seed mix together,
Roots send roots deep downwards boring;
Nature delves and builds as ever.

II

See this mind humane, serene,
Showing us the open scene
Where in woods, on meadow graze,

In steep mountain chasms yawning,
Sunset and the sunrise dawning 5
Offer God and nature praise.

III

Woods with trees and trees are teeming
Nourished, brotherly, contented,
Apt for wandering, apt for dreaming
Undisturbed and unprevented;
Where companions, though they're single, 5
Gracefully compete in presence
And to beauty's wholeness mingle,
That is joy, and that's life's essence.

IV

In the water's mirror tinted
Oak has raised itself on high,
Princely seal majestic printed
On such greening woods close by,
Sees below them its reflection, 5
In the water sees the skies:
Life enjoying to perfection,
Solitude's most precious prize.

V

Noble, grave, a half-beast lying
In recall, in contemplation,
Ponders courses multiplying,
Serving greatness his vocation.
Ah, he'd like to lose the galling 5
Burden of a hero's mentor;
Such an honour, such a calling,
Weighs down even for a centaur.

VI

Feeling grateful joy outbursting
Though it end on torment's rack,
Reaching all for which we're thirsting,
All our hearts and senses lack:
Large conception, landscape pleasing, 5

Youth steps out, in fond embrace,
Mutual each other easing,
Painful joy of love's fair grace;
All has now to you been given,
Earthly gifts, all close nearby; 10
But then yearning wants are driven
Leaving earth to rise on high.
Those are sylphs where sky is brighter,
Naiads where the fresh spring plays,
In the bathing you feel lighter, 15
Lighter still in heavenly haze;
Gliding, splashing and cascading,
Each attracts and draws you on;
Words and images are fading
But within the work's been done. 20

VII

Water calm, dark caves' recesses,
Solemn light and mountain peaks,
Strange how this our soul addresses
And with awesome import speaks.
Nature thus herself has shown, 5
Sensed by artist's eye alone.

One and All[14] (October 1821)

To find ourselves in boundless being
Who would not vanish, gladly fleeing
From all that wearies and annoys;
No ardent wants, no wild desiring,
No duties strict, no orders tiring, 5
Such self-surrender each enjoys.

World-soul, come, let your force pervade us!
To combat the world-spirit aid us
And match our powers to these high stakes.

Then sympathetic spirits guide us, 10
As gentle masters walk beside us
To him who all things made and makes.

To take what's made and then re-make it,
To fight rigidity and break it,
Eternal living action quests. 15
What never was grows real and fuller
As pure clear suns, as worlds with colour,
And in becoming never rests.

It all must move, make new creations,
First take on form, then transformations; 20
For moments it just seems held fast.
In all things life's perpetuated,
And all must be annihilated
That in existence strives to last.

Trilogy of Passion (1823–4)

To Werther

Lamented shade, once more with unsure greeting
You venture to the light of day,
Here on new-flowered meadows we are meeting;
This time you do not shrink away.
It is as if you lived when all was starting, 5
When dew upon One field our life can mend
And when the sun enraptures us in parting
With one last ray as day's drear labours end;
I stayed, you left, our fate and not our choosing,
You went before – how little you were losing. 10

The life of man seems such a splendid fate;
The day how fair, and night as well how great!
And we, in this sheer Paradise so favoured,
The sun's magnificence we've hardly savoured

When our own striving muddles and confounds us 15
Now with ourselves and now with all around us;
And neither complements the other quite,
It's dark without when all within gleams bright,
And outward bright goes dulled before my eyes,
So near – the happiness we do not prize. 20

And now we think we see! By force compelled
In love of women's image we are held:
The youth, as happy as when childhood blooms,
In spring the form of spring itself assumes,
Enrapt, amazed, who worked such spell as this? 25
He looks around, and all the world is his.
Unfettered haste impels his onward need,
No wall, no palace, nothing can impede;
As flocking birds round woodland summits fly
He hovers round his love and keeps close by, 30
And glad to leave the air, he seeks and finds
The faithful look, and this it is that binds.

But warned at first too soon and then too late
He feels his flight is checked, ensnared by fate,
To meet again is joy, to part is sore, 35
Again to meet again is joy still more,
One moment can replace long years that passed;
But farewell's patient malice wins at last.

You smile, my friend, with feeling, as is due:
A fearsome parting brought such fame for you; 40
Memorials to your piteous fate we show,
You left us here behind for weal or woe;
Then we once more were drawn into the maze
Of chartless passion's labyrinthine ways;
And we, enmeshed in pains that multiply,
At last to parting – parting is to die!
How moving always when the poet sings
To side-step death which every parting brings!
In torments snared of his half-guilt's procuring
May some god help him say what he's enduring. 50

Elegy

And while mankind is silent in its pain
A god gave me to say all that I suffer.

Now from our meeting what can be expected,
From this new day whose flowering's not yet ready?
In Paradise received, to Hell rejected;
How changeable my thoughts, my heart unsteady! –
She stands at Heaven's gate! Away with qualms! 5
She lifts you up and takes you to her arms.

So Paradise, as if you'd earned your standing,
And life forever beautiful you entered;
No need to wish, to hope, no more demanding,
The end on which your inward struggling centred; 10
As you this signal beauty contemplated
The source of all your yearning tears abated.

On what quick wings the day pursued its chases
And drove the minutes on its course swift-flighted!
The evening kiss, a seal on your embraces; 15
Until the next sun so you stay united.
Like gentle sisters hour with hour assembled
And each, though not completely, each resembled.

The kiss, the last one, sweet and anguished, shearing
A weave of love so marvellously connected. 20
Foot runs, holds back, never the threshold nearing,
As though by Cherubim in flames ejected;
Eye stares on sombre path as torments blind it,
Looks back once more, the gate stays closed behind it.

This heart is also closed, as if denying 25
That it had ever opened, no more minding
Those hours with all the constellations vying
When by her side it felt her radiance binding;
By cares, bad mood, remorse, reproach it's covered,
In sultry atmosphere oppressed and smothered. 30

But is the world not left? Those high crags shaded,
Is there not still on them a sacred presence?
The harvest not still ripening? Still unfaded
Through woods and fields the riverside's green pleasance?
And is there not on high that vastness rounding, 35
Now formlessness and now all forms abounding?

How light and delicate, how clear and tender,
From solemn clouds, seraphic, soaring high,
In lucid haze there floats an image slender,
As if herself, in blue ethereal sky; 40
So once you used to see her supreme dancing,
Of most entrancing forms the most entrancing.

But only moments dare you risk the danger
To grasp not her but mere hallucinations;
Within your heart, that's where you'll feel no stranger, 45
That's where she moves in forms and transformations;
To many One evolves through changing stages,
Thus thousandfold, and more and more engages.

The way she looked when by the gates she waited
And then on rising steps enhanced my rapture; 50
As when with one last kiss we separated
And back she ran the lastest kiss to capture:
Love's image clear and changing keeps returning,
Into this faithful heart its imprint burning,

This heart which keeps with castle-walled assurance 55
Itself for her, and her within is holding,
For her is gladdened by its own endurance,
Self-knowing only in her self-unfolding,
That feels such dear constraints are truly freeing
And only beats to thank her for all being. 60

The power to love was gone, all gone the needing
Of love's response outflowing from another;
Then hopes, bright plans, resolve, the deed succeeding,
Again the zest of living I discover!
If ever love was lover's inspiration 65
It gave in me a lovely demonstration;

And all through her! – A fearful indecision
Oppressed the mind and body, all frustrated:
Grim spectres all around the prisoned vision
In anxious heartvoid's wasteland desolated; 70
The threshold now with gleams of hope is clearing
As she in gentle sunshine is appearing.

The peace of God, more happiness bestowing
Than all our understanding – scripture tells us –
Can be compared with peace that comes from knowing 75
The loved one's presence that serenely quells us;
The heart's at rest, nought mars the deep, deep feeling
That we belong to her for life and healing.

Towards a Higher, Purer, Unknown driven
We sense our purity of heart inclining 80
In grateful self-surrender freely given,
The Evernameless-One thereby divining;
We call this: reverence! – Just so I adore her
And it is ecstasy to stand before her.

Her look, as with the sun's commanding vigour, 85
Her breath as when I sense the springtime breezes
Dissolves the icy egotistic rigour
Of self that in its wintered caverns freezes;
No self-will, no self-serving, all that's vanished,
All by her coming swept away and banished. 90

It is as if she said: 'See hour by hour
How kindly to our share in life we're bidden,
What stays from yesterday has little power,
To know what comes tomorrow is forbidden;
And if the thought of evening uneased me 95
The sun went down and I saw much that pleased me.

So do like me and look, with sense and brightly,
The moment in the eye! And no protracting!
Engage it quick, approvingly and sprightly,
For pleasure, be it loving, be it acting; 100
Be so, be always childlike, wheresoever,
So you'll be everything, defeated never.'

Well you may talk, I thought, a god did guide you,
To know the moment's favour you were gifted,
The moment any man can walk beside you 105
He feels like fortune's favourite uplifted;
I shudder at the hint of separation,
How am I helped by wisdom's education!

And now I'm far away! Take now this minute;
What's right for it? I don't know how to use it; 110
It has so much of good and beauty in it
And yet it burdens, so I must refuse it;
A longing goads me that's past all containing,
These endless tears my only help remaining.

So pour unstaunchable and flow unending! 115
But for the inward fire there's nought assuages!
Already in the storm my heart is rending
Where such grim war of death and life enrages.
With herbs the body's torments may be treated;
Without resolve and will the mind's defeated, 120

Without the thought; how give up her existence?
A thousand times her image it's defining.
It hesitates, is dragged off to the distance,
Now indistinct and now the purest shining;
But what's the use, what profit is it showing, 125
This ebb and flow, the coming and the going?

So leave me here, dear friends on all my travels!
Leave me alone in rocks and moor and heath;
Press on! For you the world itself unravels,
The sky sublime and great, wide earth beneath; 130
Examine, look, sift all the detail cluttered,
Let nature's secret haltingly be uttered.

The world's all lost, myself as well I'm losing,
I, once the favourite of the gods on high;
They tested me, for me Pandora choosing, 135

So rich in gifts, in her more dangers lie;
They urged me to that generous mouth to fate me,
They separate me and annihilate me.

Reconciliation

All passion has its pain! – Who stills the anguish
When by too great a loss the heart is riven?
Where gone the hours, so overquick to languish?
In vain to you was beauty's acme given!
The spirit drear, the muddled will's pretences; 5
The world sublime all slipping from the senses!

Then vibrant music soars on wings supernal,
A million weave of tones round tones creating
And so with beauty's overcharge eternal
All through and through man's being penetrating: 10
The eye is moistened, through a higher yearning
The power divine of tones and tears discerning.

Relieved, the supple heart then senses surely
Its beat, its eager beat, its life resurgent;
In gratitude itself it offers purely, 15
To bounteous gift makes its response convergent.
And then was sensed – oh could it last for ever! –
The double bliss of tones and love together.

The Bridegroom (1824)

At midnight's edge, I slept, by love alerted
My heart kept watch, as if it were the day;
Day came and seemed, I felt, a night deserted,
What can it be to me, bring what it may.

She was not there, my eager doings and striving 5
Were all for her alone as I withstood
The scorching hours, then what a fresh reviving
In evening's coolness! full reward and good.

The sun went down, and hand in hand united
We watched its final benediction burn, 10
And eye spoke clear to eye in silence plighted:
From Eastward, only hope, it will return.

At midnight's edge! in starlit radiance driven
Blessed dream abords the threshold where she rests.
O there at last to rest let me be given. 15
How good life is, however much it tests.

[Schiller's Remains] (1826)

In solemn charnel house I stood, surveying
The order skulls on matching skulls attested;
I called to mind the old times, gone and greying.
They stand tight-ranked, of former hates divested
And hulkish bones to mutual death once battered 5
Lie tame in this skewed mingle to be rested.
Splayed shoulder-blades! who asks, now they are scattered,
What once they carried! lissom limbs that sported,
The hand, the foot, their living join is shattered.
You tired bones, still seeking rest yet thwarted, 10
Denied the grave's deep peace, and once more driven
To day's clear light in jumbled wrack distorted;
And no man loves the husk, dried out and riven,
Despite the noble core it once was bearing.
But here to me, adept, the script was given 15
Whose sacred sense was not for common sharing
When in that press of rigid dereliction
I saw a form, a splendour past comparing.
And felt, in rotting damp and cold constriction,
As if death spilled a spring of life whose potion 20
Gave warmth and made me free in that affliction.
That form, what mystery of thrilled emotion!

Divine conception traced here, still enduring!
One look that bore me to that flooding ocean
From which augmented higher forms come pouring. 25
Mysterious vessel, oracles declaring!
Let fittingly me breach your dank immuring;
In humble hand you, treasured prize, now bearing
To open air, to sense in contemplation,
I turn with reverence to the sunlight flaring. 30
Has life for man a higher aspiration
Than God-in-Nature open to his seeing?:
Who turns to spirit matter's liquidation,
Who keeps the spirit's work in constant being.

Dornburg, September 1828 (1828)

When, in garden, valley, mountains,
Dawn through misty veils is spilling,
Colours fill the flowers as fountains,
Every utmost longing stilling,

When the ether clouding over 5
Clarity of day oppresses
And the East Wind, airy drover,
Clears the blue as sun progresses,

If you feast your eyes then, purely,
Thank the gracious great one truly, 10
Parting sun shall redden surely,
Gild the whole horizon newly.

To the Full Moon Rising (1828)

Dornburg, 25 August 1828

Will you leave me, how secure you?
When just now you were so near!
Clouds amassed in dark obscure you
And now you're no longer here.

But you sense how I am troubled, 5
And your rim returns as star!
That I'm loved you pledge redoubled
Even though my love be far.

Upwards on then! brighter brighten,
Coursing clear in glorious light! 10
Though my heart race, pain to heighten,
Overblissful is the night.

An Equation (1828)

Some flowers from the fields I sought
And took them home with many a thought;
But then from my warm hand I found
The crowns all drooping to the ground.
I put them in a fresh-filled glass 5
And what a marvel came to pass!
The heads were standing up once more,
The leaves and stalks green as before,
All flourishing as with new birth,
As if they still stood in their mother earth. 10

Just so I felt when I heard my song sung
Marvellously strange in an alien tongue.

Testament (1829)

No being can be annihilated!
In all things life's perpetuated,
Hold on to being and feel blessed!
It is eternal; lawful measure
Preserves the ever-living treasure 5
In which the universe is dressed.

The true is found and known for ever
And joins all noble minds together,
The ancient truth perceive and hold!
To the sage give thanks now, earthling, 10
Who ordered round the sun earth's circling
And orbits to the planets told.

At once in to yourself now enter
And there within you find the centre
Undoubted by the noble mind. 15
In there you'll find all regulated:
In conscience free and activated
The sun of moral life you find.

Then trust your senses for your vision,
Preventing falsity's misprision 20
By commonsense kept on the mark.
With insight fresh observing blithely
Then wander certainly and lithely
About this world's endowered park.

Let moderation's joys sustain you 25
And reason's presence entertain you
Where life is life's felicity.
The past's forever re-created,
The future here anticipated,
The moment is eternity. 30

And finally when you've achieved it
And in each fibre you perceive it:
In fruitfulness is truth's true test,
You judge society's ruling passion,
It carries on in its own fashion, 35
And find the smallest company best.

And just as to the life secluded
Philosophers and poets are mooded
And thus their work of love was cast,
You too will seek high grace and merits: 40
For to prefigure noble spirits
Is a vocation unsurpassed.

Chinese-German Hours and Seasons

(1827–30)

I

Tell us mandarins enquiring,
Sated rulers, servants tiring,
Tell, what's left us except yearning
To be quit when spring's around us,
Shaking off the North that bound us, 5
And by ponds, on grass reclining,
Gaily drink, write wit and learning,
Cup on cup, brushed strokes entwining?

II

Pure as candles, lilies' whiteness,
Starlike, bowed in modest station,
From the middle heart shines brightness,
Red-hemmed glow of inclination.

Thus narcissi prematurely 5
Bloom along the garden border.
Only they can know, though, surely
Whom they wait for ranked in order.

III

From the meadow sheep are leaving,
There it lies, a purest green;
Soon though, Paradise conceiving,
It will bloom with flowering sheen.

Light of hope is permeating 5
Outspread veils of misty shrouds:
Wants fulfilled, sun celebrating,
Happiness, break through the clouds!

IV

The peacock's cry is horrid, but his call
Reminds me that his plumage is celestial,
And so for me his cry is not too bestial.
But Indian Geese are not the same at all,
Listening to them is quite impossible: 5
They're horrid, and their cry is just not tolerable.

V

When evening sun's gold rays pour down
Resplendently unfurl your desires,
Revolve your bold-eyed train and crown
And match him with your boastful fires.
He seeks what's flowering in the green, 5
What's in the garden blue-sky vaulted;
And where there's lovers to be seen
He knows he sees what's most exalted.

VI

The cuckoo and the nightingale
Cast spells so spring may settle,
But summer thrusts and soon makes them fail
With the thistle and the nettle.
On my tree now the leaves' light weft 5
Is densely concentrated
Through which for love's most lovely theft
My eye once penetrated;
Now lattice, doors, and roof bright-crowned

Are covered altogether; 10
That place my searching eye once found
Remains my East forever.

VII

Than fairest day she was more fair
And so I beg your pardon
That I recall her everywhere
And more so in a garden.
It was a garden, she drew near 5
And so her favour rendered;
I feel it still and mind it dear
And stay to her surrendered.

VIII

Twilight down from high has drifted,
What was near's already far;
First, though, high above is lifted
Graced in light the evening star!
All on imprecision verges, 5
To the heights the mists slow snake;
Darkness into blackness merges
Mirrored in the resting lake.

Now I sense the moonlight presses
Ardent in the evening sky; 10
Slender willows' branching tresses
Jest upon the wave nearby.
Luna's quivering spell is glowing
Where the shadows play and dart,
Coolness through the eye is flowing 15
Soothingly into the heart.

IX

Only now do we know the rosebud at last,
Now when the time for roses has passed;
On the stem a laggard's shining still,
Singly the world of flowers to fulfil.

X

Most beautiful of all you are acclaimed,
In the realm of flowers as queen you are named;
Unanswerable general testament,
Banishing conflict, marvellous event!
You truly are, not merely so appear, 5
In you belief agrees with vision clear;
Yet science strives and struggles, never tires,
For law and cause, for Why and How enquires.

XI

'Theorising's reprehensible,
I fear its snares and fret
Where nothing stays and all things flee,
Where disappears the thing we see;
Grey fears incomprehensible 5
Enmesh me in their net.' –
Fear not! The indestructible
In the eternal law is set
By which the rose and lily be.

XII

'Man's old dreaming here disposes,
Trees you talk to, fondle roses,
Girls and sages you're excluding;
That won't do, for ever brooding,
That's why now together banding 5
By your side your friends are standing,
Help for you and us, we're thinking,
Is colour, brush, on green lawns drinking.'

XIII

Why now disturb my quiet elation?
Leave me with my wine alone.
With others one gets education
But inspiration on one's own.

XIV

'Well now! Before we dash away
Haven't you something wise to say?'

Pining for Far and Future is assuaged
If here and now you're solidly engaged.

[The Speechless Pain . . .]

(date unknown)

The speechless pain has said its part,
Clearer blue and bluer clears the air,
The golden lyre, look, hovering there,
Come, my old friend, come to my heart.

Notes

1. Satyros or The Idolised Demon of the Woods: A dramatic satire on the itinerant soap-box preachers of the time promoting their own personal sects, and also on the over-simplistic followers of Rousseau's call for a return to nature.

2. The New Amadis: Amadis is a hero of fifteenth- and sixteenth-century Iberian romance. Prince Pipi and Princess Fish probably derive from French fairy tales.

3. Untitled – from Egmont: In Goethe's play on the Dutch struggle for independence from Spain, *Egmont* (published 1787), this song is sung by the hero's beloved Klärchen, a young bourgeois woman who, after Egmont is imprisoned and sentenced to death by the Spanish, commits suicide.

4. To the Spirit of Johannes Secundus: Johannes Secundus was a sixteenth-century Dutch poet who wrote in Latin, author of a series of passionate sensual poems called *Basia* ('kisses'). Goethe retained a kindred feeling for him throughout his life.

5. Roman Elegies V, l.20: The reference is not to the political triumvirates of Pompey, Crassus, and Caesar or to Mark Antony, Lepidus, and Octavian, but to the Latin love poets Catullus, Propertius, and Tibullus, who were inspired in the same way as the poet of these elegies.

6. Withheld Venetian Epigrams XLI, l.6: In the story told by Rabelais and Lafontaine, Hans Carvel dreamt that he was given a ring which, so long as he wore it, would ensure his wife's fidelity. He woke to find around his finger a ring of a different kind.

7. World Soul: The poem addresses the enthusiastic proponents of the Romantic idealist philosophy of F. W. J. Schelling (1775–1854).

8. Sonnet Cycle XI, l.7: The allusion is to Wilhelm von Schütz's play *Lacrimas* (1803), which uses an array of Romantic verse forms.

9. Sonnet Cycle XVII: The riddle in this poem on the words *Herz* ('heart'), *lieb* ('dear', 'beloved'), and *herzlieb* ('dearest' or 'darling') cannot be reproduced in English. The sonnet came about as a result of a competition between Goethe, the Romantic playwright Zacharias Werner, and the classicist F. W. Riemer to compose a sonnet in honour of Wilhelmine Herzlieb, the eighteen-year-old ward of the Jena bookseller Frommann.

10. The Diary: Tibullus, *Elegies*, I.v.39–40.

11. The Diary, l.136: 'iste' is the Latin pronoun 'this (one)' or 'that (one)'. Later in the poem it is called 'Meister Iste', translated here as 'Master' in the sense of the craft-guilds as one who has skill and authority. A literal translation 'Master That One' can also carry in English the connotation of an unruly boy.

12. Epirrhema: In Greek drama the *epirrhema* is a verse that follows a chorus and in which the chorus leader addresses the audience. An *antepirrhema* is a second such verse.

13. Eve of St Nepomuk: Nepomuk, a fourteenth-century Vicar General of Prague, was drowned in the Moldau on the orders of Wenceslas IV because he opposed royal interference in clerical prerogatives and, according to legend, because he refused to betray to the King the Queen's confidences given to him under the seal of the confessional.

14. One and All: Some years after this poem was written some public misunderstanding of its implications prompted Goethe to respond with 'Testament' (p. 93).